When Jesus Shows Up In Skinny Jeans

From knowing about Jesus to knowing Jesus—a personal testimony to challenge and inspire you.

EMILY SMITH

©2024 by Emily Smith

Published by Emily Smith, 2024.

All rights reserved. No part of this publication may be reproduced, stored in a retrieval system, or transmitted in any form or by any means—for example, electronic, photocopy, recording—without the prior written permission of the publisher. The only exception is brief quotations in printed reviews.

For information about wholesale, special discounts for bulk purchases, and to have Emily Smith speak at your event, please contact Emily at emily@designedtobeministries.org

Print ISBN 979-8-9907503-1-9
EBook ISBN 979-8-9907503-0-2

Scripture marked NIV is taken from the Holy Bible, New International Version®, NIV® Copyright ©1973, 1978, 1984, 2011 by Biblica, Inc.® Used by permission. All rights reserved worldwide.

Scripture marked MSG is taken from The Message, copyright © 1993, 2002, 2018 by Eugene H. Peterson.

Scripture marked KJV is taken from the King James version of the Bible and are in the public domain.

Scripture marked ESV is taken from the English Standard version of the Holy Bible, English Standard Version. ESV® Text Edition: 2016. Copyright © 2001 by Crossway Bibles, a publishing ministry of Good News Publishers.

Scripture marked NASB is taken from New American Standard Bible®, Copyright © 1960, 1971, 1977, 1995, 2020 by The Lockman Foundation. All rights reserved.

Scripture marked NKJV is taken from the New King James Version®. Copyright © 1982 by Thomas Nelson. Used by permission. All rights reserved.

Scripture marked NET is taken from NET Bible® copyright ©1996-2017 by Biblical Studies Press, L.L.C. http://netbible.com All rights reserved.

Scripture marked NRSV is taken from New Revised Standard Version Bible: Anglicised Edition, copyright © 1989, 1995 the Division of Christian Education of the National Council of the Churches of Christ in the United States of America. Used by permission. All rights reserved.

Acknowledgments

The generosity of many brought this book from a desire in my heart to being released into the world. It has been a labor of love for ten years, and many have shown love and given inspiration throughout my entire journey.

I would like to thank my husband, Rolf Smith, who patiently walked the foundational journey that produced this book. You loved me through it all. I am grateful for your design and formatting skills, objectivity, patience, and willingness to use all those gifts to help me become an author. I love you.

My family, Hannah and Rylan Smith, George and Susan Worthley, Mark Worthley, and Amy Worthley were part of developing this testimony within me, even if they did not know it. Thank you for your love and support in life and throughout this writing journey. To Amy, in particular, thank you for inviting me on the trip to Cuba in 2013. Because you listened and obeyed, and then I listened and obeyed, Jesus took the open door into my life and brought His mercy, grace, and miraculous power. It changed everything for me and my family. Years later, I have a testimony of countless lives also transformed by the love of Jesus, and it all roots back to your simple act of obedience.

Through my writing journey, even before I knew it was to be a published book, God placed a handful of men and women into my life. Each one walked alongside me, spoke encouragement and wisdom, and helped me see how to carry out this vision. They each hold a special place in my heart. Thank you Lynn Cowell, Sandra Tolsma, Kim Wolfe, Skip Strauchman, Scott Ladd, and Tara Hollis.

I would not have been able to accomplish any of this work without the incredible vision and support of my editors. Rebecca Cooper copyedited this book, and Steve Norman completed my reader experience editing. Rebecca and Steve went above and beyond, using their editing skills to help develop this book in a way that I could not have done alone. They cut through redundancies and challenged my theology to help align the truth of God's word with the power of my testimony and to keep it all relatable. I am grateful for their vision, gentle correction, and encouragement.

My friend, Annette Bourland, Bourland Strategic Advisors, has supported me through her gifts of strategy and industry wisdom. By blessing me with her talents, Annette has helped further my journey toward publication. I am beyond grateful for her kindness, leadership, affirming words, and patient teaching. Thank you.

The Holy Spirit named this book When Jesus Shows Up In Skinny Jeans. Since that moment, I knew the cover would come from another source. I am grateful that God chose Steve Norman's daughter, Grace Norman, a college student to bring forth the inspiration, for my daughter Hannah who helped refine our approach, and for my man, Rolf, who brought it home.

To my beta readers and prayer warriors, some already named and some listed below, you are a gift. Your faithful pursuit of the Lord on my behalf, and behalf of this book, has not been in vain. I am grateful for the moments when you shared how God was leading you to pray, and for the knowledge that, even when I didn't hear, you regularly sought Him. Thank you for walking with me, making this a part of your prayer life, and your faithful friendship. Heidi VanderWal, Belinda Ungrey, Katrina Lockard, Audrey Strickland, and Pamela LaLonde.

Table Of Contents

Introduction 9

Chapter 1
Meeting Jesus in a Dream 17

Chapter 2
Developing a Sensitivity to the Holy Spirit 37

Chapter 3
Canceling Fear and Taking Up Authority 51

Chapter 4
Pursuing the Fruit of the Spirit: Love, Kindness, Joy, and Peace 63

Chapter 5
Still Pursuing the Fruit of the Spirit: Patience, Faithfulness, Goodness, Self-Control, and Gentleness 85

Chapter 6
Appreciating Anointing and Baptism 111

Chapter 7
Growing in Confession, Repentance, and Responsive Obedience 127

Chapter 8
Understanding How Satan Works 145

Chapter 9
Conclusion 155

Introduction

Since an invitation to go to Cuba in 2013, I have been encountering a whole new experience of Jesus I never knew was available to me. It includes things like identifying the lies I was believing about myself, learning to confess and repent, realizing Jesus wanted a relationship with me, and then learning how to participate in that relationship. I really had no idea what I was doing, nor did I understand how walking it out would bless the trajectory of my life. I just knew that the more I stepped into it, deep down, something in me felt better, lighter, freer than it did before. It felt right, and the feeling of defeat I had been living with was replaced with confidence, encouragement, and empowerment.

Today, I am blessed to own and operate a ministry with a storefront that is God's assignment for me. It's a women's clothing and accessory boutique that is a part of changing the world, one purchase at a time. If you knew me ten years ago, you might have a hard time believing that, given my fashion history, I would ever open a boutique. It is only God, and it all started with Jesus showing up in skinny jeans. I am blessed by this opportunity to share my testimony with you, and I hope it opens the door for you to encounter Jesus.

When Jesus Shows Up in Skinny Jeans is a representation of my personal testimony of going from a place of knowing about Jesus to knowing and living life with and for Jesus. As part of the Lord's call on my life, He prompted me to start a class called "Designed To Be." It is a class that covers the depth of this content over the course of two years. The book version is meant to reach those who could not take the class but desire the same truth. Every group of women who has come through Designed To Be class has had a common experience: The Lord was faithful to bring the lesson into a moment of their life when they needed the lesson. He faithfully met them every time. I believe Jesus will show up for you, the reader, as well. I invite you to do business with God, dive in and seek Him with intentionality, as you read it. Don't just gloss over the text; use this as an opportunity to go deeper with Him and to come out of the mediocrity in your faith.

> **I never had much fashion sense. When skinny jeans first hit the fashion scene, I probably felt like many of you. How was I going to put my regular size body into irregularly tiny jeans? Do you remember how you felt when you first saw someone in skinny jeans? It may be similar to how you have felt in recent years with the return of wide legs. I had this exact thought: "Not gonna do it!" But when I realized they were here to stay, I warmed to the idea and eventually bought a pair.**

It is not lost on me that the imagery of Jesus in skinny jeans conflicts with religious thinking. It is intentional. I am not religious. Neither is Jesus. He has no interest in religion. He is motivated by His love for the Father and is faithful to that love. I am living a life trying to be faithful to Jesus as I get to know Him personally through our raw, authentic, and intimate relationship (Ephesians 1:15–19 MSG). Many Christians know about Jesus but have not established a relationship with Jesus. Religious and doctrine-oriented ways of thinking are partially responsible for that. Religion and doctrine are not why Jesus came. He came for salvation and for faith. He hopes for relationship with you, right here and right now.

In 2012, I began exiting a lifetime of mediocre Christianity and knowing about Jesus. I was invited to experience more of Jesus by attending a mission trip in Cuba. I wanted to give a hard no to that invitation. I was in a place where I wanted more Jesus in my life, but I was also afraid of what that would look like. I thought, "Jesus is going to expose all my old sins." It was this thought that almost won over in my mind, but eventually, Jesus won in my heart, and I agreed to go. My yes came out of a place of beginning to desire Jesus more than my ridiculous secret fear that He would expose all my stuff.

After I agreed to go, my experience of getting to know Jesus was amplified by a powerful dream. In the dream, I encountered an intense fear that something terrible was going to happen to my children while I was away. This dream fear was paralyzing and aligned with the fear I was actually living in as I was preparing to go on this mission trip. In both the dream and my real life, I kept thinking, "Something bad is going to happen, and there is nothing I can do about it."

This dream came just a few years after skinny jeans entered mainstream fashion. Jesus used skinny jeans as an opportunity to demonstrate to me that He cares about the details of our life and meets us right where we are. Without any grandeur or any hesitation, Jesus walked right into the center of my dream, wearing skinny jeans. Even more remarkable was that His presence in the dream completely canceled the fear. The very instant He entered the scene, my fear broke, and peace consumed me. And, in pure Jesus style, when I woke from this dream, I was fully aware that He had also broken the fear that was pursuing me in real life and replaced it with His peace.

Although I had spent my life in church, this was the first time I had experienced the direct effect of the presence of my Savior and Lord, Jesus Christ, exchanging negative feelings for His peace. His peace not only affected my perspective about going on the mission trip but also created a longing within me to experience more of Him.

Jesus is inviting you to experience more of Him. He desires to be involved in the details of your circumstances and wants you to encounter His peace within them. He desires to affect all your circumstances and exchange your negatives for His positives. No matter what you have done or what has been done to you, He loves you and freely offers this peace to you. All of heaven is cheering you on to say yes.

John 14:6–7 (MSG) says, "Jesus said, 'I am the Road, also the Truth, also the Life. No one gets to the Father apart from me. If you really knew me, you would know my Father as well. From now on, you do know him. You've even seen him!'" Jesus in skinny jeans refers to the authenticity of who Jesus is. It's a demonstration of Jesus' heart for you and His desire to be invited into the mix of your life so you can know Him, rather than just know about Him. He wants to tear down the walls that have been put up to keep Him at a distance. He longs for you to experience a relationship with Him and to let Him show up in ways you understand even through the rawness of your circumstances.

Mainstream fashion is currently shifting away from skinny jeans to wide-leg pants. Although many women still love them and look amazing in them, Gen Z has decided that skinny jeans are no longer cool. There is a juxtaposition between this fashion shift and faith in Jesus. As a culture, we spend a lot of energy trying to keep up with changing fashion and whatever the new norm is.

However, those changes in fashion don't always work for your unique design. Trends don't always work well with your personal style or align with what's most flattering for your body shape. Some of us look and feel our best in skinny jeans, while others can rock a wide leg, and still others can wear both styles confidently. When styles in mainstream fashion change, the person who prefers the previous style may be left feeling as if they no longer fit in, what they prefer wearing is insufficient, or somehow their personal style is being compromised.

We cannot take what happens in the fashion industry and apply it to Jesus. The circumstances of the world and the things around us will always change, but Jesus never changes. The fashion industry may decide that skinny jeans are out, but the beauty of a faith-based relationship with Jesus is that it is not one size fits all. Your relationship with Him will look distinctly different from someone else's because of how you were uniquely created. Part of what makes Jesus so amazing is how He pursues and encourages us in alignment with our individuality. Faith in Jesus is about getting to know who Jesus wants to be for you in every circumstance you face. His pursuit of you is always constant, and nothing will change that. Jesus is always the perfect fit for you.

Do you feel like your faith is "off the rack" and following the trends of culture rather than immersed in the unique ways Jesus wants you to encounter Him? Is your Christianity mediocre? Do you desire something more with Jesus, and are you ready to grow in ways others around you are not? No matter where you are today, you are not meant to dwell there. The truth of Jesus is that He always has more for you, and He is always desiring to start pouring more into your life! Jesus is wooing you into a relationship with Him, and He longs to show up in skinny jeans for you. Your relationship with Jesus is meant to be cultivated, to keep maturing, and to become more intimate throughout your life. If you desire that, but it's not happening for you, it's because something is in the way. Jesus desires to lovingly partner with you to reveal and resolve whatever that is.

What separates those who mature in their faith and experience Jesus from those who do not is the decision to pursue an intimate relationship with Him, and a willingness to receive what He offers. He is always pursuing you and has a desire for you to grow in relationship with Him, but your experience of Him is up to you. Are you going to pursue more of Jesus and let Him become Lord of your life, or are you going to stay right where you are and just hope for a different outcome?

Years after my dream, God transformed my obedience and pursuit of Jesus into both a class I taught, "Designed To Be," and this book. This book is a progressive revelation of God, in chronological order, through my personal testimony of going from knowing about Jesus to knowing Jesus intimately. If you decide to stick around and keep reading, you'll progressively encounter some life-changing truths I've discovered. I am confident He will give you the opportunity to apply what you're learning to your circumstances in real time.

Change is hard, and this book is designed to bring forth change in your life. Not change just for the sake of change, but heart and mind transformation brought on by an awareness of Jesus Christ within you. He longs to bring you out of mediocrity and into the fullness of who He wants to be for you, right here and right now. That cannot happen without change. When you finish reading, my hope is that you'll have a deeper astonishment of Jesus, a desire to walk more intimately with Him and the Holy Spirit and a deeper understanding of your identity in Christ, who He is and who He wants to be for you. More of Jesus is available to you. I hope you stay.

CHAPTER 1

Meeting Jesus in a Dream

I was invited by my sister to join her as she led a group of women on a mission trip to Cuba. The invitation came as I was just starting to re-engage with Jesus. I had been committed to church, youth group, and Bible studies all my life, but in the years immediately prior to this invitation I had paid significantly less attention to Jesus. As a result, I had engaged in sin but had not yet confessed, repented and dealt with the consequences of those sins. I was hiding from God about them and hoped they would just fade away by going through all the religious motions, showing up to church on Sunday and attending women's Bible study. I was just doing it out of muscle memory. There was absolutely no authenticity in me. I was putting my comfortable, yet dysfunctional, sin desires above Jesus, yet showing up to all the church events to be sure it looked externally like I had it all together and was committed to my religion. After all, that's what we're supposed to do, right? Keep all appearances as if it's all good.

I was just beginning to come into a place where I was over that way of life, and I wanted Jesus more than I wanted the dysfunction of sin in my life. Jesus seized the opportunity to win my heart and brought forth the invitation to Cuba. I said yes to the trip, but it was not an easy yes. I was freaking out about it. I had a relentless fear that Jesus was going to expose the old sin in my life. I believed that He was going to do something like put me on a stage and make me publicly confess. I had never in my life seen this kind of thing happen and had no precedent for why I would believe this, but it was a constant fear that I clearly felt was trying to deter me from going to Cuba.

There was much I didn't understand. I wasn't really sure how things worked with God. Despite a lifetime of church exposure, I had no idea how to confess or what repentance was, and even thinking about forgiveness felt overwhelming, so I quickly shut them down. Since I didn't understand any of it, my limitless imagination gave life to fears and what-ifs.

In the midst of not knowing how anything with God worked, I also could not figure out how something within me could so deeply desire God while simultaneously something else within me was freaking out about the idea of pursuing God. God won this internal battle, and with my decision to go, I began the process of preparing for the trip. It didn't take long for me to realize that my yes to God was going to usher in my exit from a lifetime of mediocre Christianity.

I also had no idea that God was going to use this trip to plant some seeds in me that would not only bring me back to Cuba for watering, but also would ignite a desire within me for something He designed in me that I had no clear idea about yet. This something from God involved not only my exit from a lifetime of mediocre Christianity but also an exit from a lifetime of mediocre fashion. I was unknowingly in the very early stages of changing career paths, stepping into God's assignment for me to open a ministry with a storefront, and stepping out of my Doc Martin's and khaki cargo pants.

Preparation for my first trip to Cuba involved things like journaling. Ugh. I was not a journaler. I considered it something that just took time and was not valuable. What would you do with it when the journal was full? Put it in a box and save it? Toss it? Burn it? It just didn't make sense to me. But the very first encouragement my sister gave me was, "Start journaling what God teaches you." She went on to tell me that it would come back around at some point and it's hard to remember all that God says and does. In full representation of how I felt about journaling, I reluctantly found an old paperback notepad we already had in the house. I'm certain it was a freebie from some event, and every five pages or so, there was an old drawing from my children or practice alphabet letters. There were no lines on the pages and only about thirty pages total, but I started.

Preparation also involved a new kind of interaction with Jesus. He began meeting me through my dreams and with visions while I prayed. My entire life, I had been a very vivid dreamer, always very detailed and with wild activities. I recalled my dreams all the time, but I never knew that dreams were a way Jesus might try to talk to me, so I never gave them any attention. Until, that is, somewhere in the process of preparing for Cuba, my dreams dropped out like purple corduroy pants did in the late '80s. The lack of dreams was significant enough that it reached a journaling level of importance, and I wrote about it in my small journal. I thought, "It must be from God because I'm really aware of it."

Years earlier, I began getting consumed with fear. I had fear about everything: my career, my family, my marriage, my economy, my future, my old sin, my relationship with God. Everything had fear attached to it. I had no idea how to deal with fear, so I did what I had always done with things that I didn't know what to do with: I buried it. I swept everything under the rug and hoped that in leaving it alone that it would eventually just go away. It never did, but I spent years in that perpetual cycle of dysfunction because I had no idea how to resolve fear.

When I would bury the fear, it would lessen for a while, but I was always aware it was still lurking somewhere deep down just waiting to mess with me.

In the dormant seasons, I would just keep doing what I was doing, and I would forget to go deeper to deal with the root of the fear. I wouldn't remember to process the fear until the next time it came out of dormancy. It is so hard to deal with fear in its active state, so the perpetual cycle would just continue. Does this kind of fear-driven anxiety sound familiar to you? It's pretty common. There are entire industries and careers built around this perpetual cycle.

The season of preparation for Cuba is where fear came out of its dormancy. It was clear to me that fear did not want me to pursue Jesus or go to Cuba and encounter Jesus' presence. I could feel in my body that fear was trying to intimidate me, doing anything it could to keep me from going through with what I knew Jesus was prompting in me. The internal battle perpetuated for months, and it was only because I was at the end of the comfortable dysfunction of my life that I kept pressing in toward Jesus. Even as the months went on, I didn't understand what it was. I just knew deep down that this new thing happening in me was better than where I had been.

Jesus responded to these fear attacks by using my dreams to demonstrate His authority over fear. After months of having no dreams, one morning, as I started my day, standing in front of the mirror with a mouth full of toothpaste, a dream fully returned to my mind. I cannot explain it more than telling you that every fiber of my being knew this dream was from Jesus, and He had something to say to me about it. After I changed my shirt due to the toothpaste that flew out of my mouth when I remembered the dream, I texted my sister because somehow I knew I had to share this dream with her.

The dream opened on a black-and-white scene at night. I was standing in a large circle with my sister and a group of women I did not know. As we stood in the circle, an overwhelming presence of fear consumed me. It was a chest-crushing kind of fear, like an oppressive, heavy weight, and it made me want to run away. I had tremendous fear that something bad was going to happen to me or to my family while I was in Cuba, and that there was nothing I could do about it. I kept feeling like I shouldn't go to Cuba, and if I don't go, maybe this horrible thing won't happen. In the center of the circle of women, there were a bunch of wild dogs. They were fighting amongst themselves, and within the black-and-white scene, I could see their red blood. Fear loomed heavier as I contemplated this bad thing that was going to happen to my family while simultaneously watching this horribly violent dogfight. Into the circle walked a man. I could not see his face, but he was wearing skinny jeans and a tank top.

Instantly, when this man entered the circle, fear left, and peace overwhelmed me. I immediately felt the profound shift and the release of the oppressive, heavy weight. At that moment, I understood for the first time ever the difference between fear and peace. That was profound for me, as I had never contemplated that I didn't know the difference between fear and peace. That heavy weight of fear that left my body was replaced with an unfamiliar confidence in God and a sense of His authority, love, and goodness. I didn't understand how, I just knew it was real and that I was marked by this experience. As I recalled the dream, I recalled the physical release of the weight and could actually feel the lightness in my physical body.

My sister was more mature in her faith than I was, and I knew God sometimes brought her interpretations of dreams. Somehow, I had confidence He would do that with this dream in order to answer all my burning questions. God did show up, but not necessarily how I thought He would. Through conversation and prayer with my sister, God revealed that the man in skinny jeans who came into the circle was Christ Jesus. He showed up, not wearing a fancy priestly robe or some other kind of flashy royal garment, but rather, wearing the most simplistic, unassuming, and relatable garment of the time. This dream occurred smack at the peak of skinny jean popularity.

Jesus has always surrendered His royalty for the sake of relationship. The displacement of fear in exchange for the peace of His presence affirmed His authority over fear as well as His provision and protection over me, my family, and those going on the trip with me. In the fullness of His real, raw, authentic, lacking-in-nothing self, Jesus stepped right into my circumstance and met me right where I was.

I continued in prayer about this dream for several days, and Jesus went on to reveal things I had never understood before. He taught me that the wild dogs represented Satan's demons, and that they were fighting amongst themselves in the spirit realm because they couldn't get to me or my family because we were so protected by the presence of Jesus. I came to understand that Jesus entered the circle because I invited Him. He had been waiting for my invitation to get involved in my life. When I began to pursue Him and invited Him into my circumstances, Jesus willingly entered and met me right where I was. He displaced all the negatives in exchange for His positives. And because Jesus was welcomed, Satan (fear) had to acknowledge Jesus' authority and leave.

I confess that, initially, I fully expected some kind of literal interpretation, like "Wild dogs want to eat you, Emily." But instead, it was all about Jesus' goodness and authority over it all. It was a revelation of how Jesus had gone so far ahead of me, and through my obedience to His prompts, Satan's plans for me were being frustrated. This new understanding began to answer the conflict I had been feeling between my body freaking out about going to Cuba and something peaceful deep within beckoning me to go.

This was also my first real awareness that there are actual demons Satan controls, and he uses them to control, intimidate, strike fear, and accomplish his evil objectives. I always kind of knew there were demons, but I had never been taught about them, so I never really acknowledged it because it felt so intimidating and over the top. The whole subject is avoided by many Christians for some of the same reasons.

Several new desires stirred in me in the weeks after this dream. Not only did I now know there was a difference between fear and peace and good and evil, but I also knew I wanted that peace in my life all the time. I wanted to know how to have peace even if horrible things were happening around me. I didn't want the fear and what ifs to rule my life anymore. I tasted freedom in Christ Jesus, and I wanted more. I wanted to know who this Jesus who I never met at church really is. I wanted this kind of excitement in my relationship with Jesus all the time. I wanted to understand this God who would show up in skinny jeans and how He made me feel all the things I felt just by being in His presence.

I also wanted to understand His authority over the enemy. The release of the fear I had been living in was so profound. I wanted to understand how that happened. I wanted to experience more of the presence of Jesus in my life. I began asking Jesus in prayer to protect what He had done in me and telling Him that I didn't ever want to have fear like that again. I'd ask Him, "Please take this fear, Jesus. It's too much for me." In response to my pursuit after Him, He met me daily, whispering, "Peace be with you." It was the exact reminder of His calm that I needed in the midst of feeling like I was swimming upstream with attacks and doubts. When I stopped, sought His face, and received what He was offering me, the distress would leave, and I would return to His peace. It was like He was using my life circumstances to teach me how to stay in peace. I had tasted it, I knew the difference, and now I was learning how to dwell in it.

Isaiah 26:3 (NIV) says, "You will keep in perfect peace those whose minds are steadfast, because they trust in you." All believers have the promise of salvation in Jesus. The church as a whole does a really great job of telling people about His authority to save us. We're excellent at telling the salvation story where salvation is the immediate goal. Jesus made a way for our salvation and forgiveness, but that's not all He did. This approach toward saving souls isn't wrong, but sadly, new Christians are not well shepherded into learning and understanding about coming under the lordship of Jesus. As a result, many Christians live a lifetime never knowing Jesus as Lord of their life. Rather, they hold Jesus at a distance but close enough to pull Him back in when they need the promise or when things go bad—not really close enough to change anything about the way they live or think. In stopping at salvation, Christians miss the excitement of life in relationship with Jesus the Christ, our Lord and Savior.

If you're holding Him at arm's length, this is bringing you only a mediocre experience of Christianity. He longs to have an intimate relationship with you, where you pursue Him, invite His presence into your circumstances, and let Him be part of your life. Like any relationship, you need to engage with the other person. The development of your intimate relationship with Him is designed to be a journey that deeply represents the kingdom of God, Jesus' holiness, and His promises for you, on earth as it is in heaven. In order for Jesus to step into His role as Lord of your life, you need to invite Him, and then you have to actually let Him do it.

Religion and doctrine were essential components of the old covenant with God before Jesus served as the final sacrifice for our transgressions. On this side of the cross, I believe religion represents external ceremonial behavior without any real heart or mind transformation by Jesus. Regarding doctrine, I am referring to its use in Matthew 16:12, where it roots to the Hebrew translation meaning "teaching, that which is taught," by those who are not motivated by Jesus or the Holy Spirit (the Pharisees and of the Sadducees). In my personal experience, and what I have seen through Designed To Be Ministry, religion and doctrine continue to hold significant importance, and thereby hold many Christians in mediocre Christianity. I am not suggesting that you shouldn't attend church or get involved with conventional religion. The Lord is clear that we need fellowship and community in faith (Matthew 18:20, Acts 2:44). However, the global church is divided on the issue of religion and doctrine, and it's not because Jesus is divided. He is not confused. He came to do a new thing, and His entire ministry on earth repeats that message. Religion and doctrine didn't get it then and still don't get it today. Religious and doctrinal mindsets conflict with faith and relationship, and are actually not supposed to have any place in the new covenant with Jesus. Religion and doctrine pay attention to what God did (in Jesus' time on earth) and what God is going to do (the future promise of salvation). Religion and doctrine ignore what God is doing right here and right now, today (Christ in you).

There are limitations attached to religion and doctrine that encourage believers to justify the lack of Jesus in their lives here and now. Religion and doctrine claim the grace of Jesus but still refer to people as sinners, causing us to believe the lie that we are not worthy of experiencing and enjoying Him.

His grace is fully true and available to you, and it is by His grace that God declares you righteous through your faith in Christ. When you are in Christ, you can confess your sins, repent, and receive God's forgiveness because of Jesus' sacrifice. He willingly pours out His grace over and over again when you confess and repent. It has no limits when your confession is authentic (1 John 1:9). And, in this symbiotic relationship, experiencing His grace causes a response of more confession and repentance because you simply begin to desire more of His love for you and less of everything that kept you from Him. In grace, there is a supernatural power that comes alive in us that causes us to not sin because of His goodness, not our own. Grace is not permission to keep sinning, but we also don't need to wait to come to Him until we are clean of our own accord. It simply won't ever happen. God cleans us through our act of surrender and His imputed grace.

Many in the church misunderstand grace. Some think grace is freedom to stay in the prison of sin, when in truth, it's grace that breaks us free from the strongholds of sin. I have heard many teach on and define grace as undeserved favor. John 1:14 (NIV) says, "The Word became flesh and made his dwelling among us. We have seen his glory, the glory of the one and only Son, who came from the Father, full of grace and truth." This means that Jesus has grace. Undeserved grace is not warranted, merited, or earned. How is it possible that grace is undeserved if Jesus, who was the spotless lamb sacrificed for us, has grace? Defining grace like that confuses and spirals the misunderstanding of grace among believers.

Hebrews 4:16 (NIV) says, "Let us then [fearlessly, confidently and boldly] approach God's throne of grace with confidence, so that we may receive mercy and find grace to help us in our time of need." The Lord God Almighty is the God of mercy. Mercy is about your past failures, shortcomings, and sins. Mercy is not about today. Grace is about today and your future. Grace is well timed, coming just when we need it and in real time! I've heard many say, "Take the mercy, accept the help of grace." I believe that grace is the empowering presence of God that pours over us and enables us to step up into all the things He designed us to be.

Since our sin nature causes us to need Jesus, many Christians believe that heaven refers to us as sinners, but Jesus doesn't call you sinner. He calls you a saint. The righteousness of Christ gets put in you when you come into salvation and under the lordship of Jesus. Since you're in Christ, and Christ is in you, when the Father looks at you, He sees you through the lens of Jesus. Therefore, He sees the righteousness of His Son, Jesus, in you. He only sees your potential in Christ Jesus, not your mistakes.

Traditional religion and doctrine views saints very differently from what Jesus taught. Many theologies classify saints as a special kind of believer, one who has done noteworthy deeds. Life in Christ Jesus is not based on performance, therefore, heavenly titles are not assigned according to performance. These traditional religious views of saints are man-made doctrine and a way of thinking that is the opposite of kingdom thinking. The ministry of Christ referred to saints as those set apart for kingdom work.

Ephesians 4:12 (ESV) says, "to equip the saints for the work of ministry, for building up the body of Christ." God the Father refers to all who are in Christ as saints. If you're in Christ, and God calls those in Christ saints, and you instead refer to yourself as a sinner, does it not diminish who the Father, your Creator, the Lord God Almighty, says you are? Of course it does. If you believe you're one thing, but God's Word says you are the complete opposite, of course believing the lie will interfere with your understanding about who God is and who God says you are.

Your identity is in Christ Jesus. Believing you're something other than who God says you are introduces all sorts of wrong thinking and behaviors that draw you further away from relationship with

Jesus. John 5:17 (NIV) says, "In his defense Jesus said to them, 'My Father is always at his work to this very day, and I too am working.'" Jesus is right here, right now. He is not interested in your religion and doctrine. He wants a relationship with you. He is only interested in developing your faith in Him. Religion and faith, while often used synonymously, are not the same thing. Jesus wants you to know Him (faith), not just know about Him (religion).

You might find yourself asking, "How do I get out of religion and grow my faith?" I'm glad you asked! There are some clear themes in Scripture that teach us how! Consider with me first, though, just for a moment, that if there were things you just read that you didn't know before, that there will be other things about Jesus and God you also didn't know. Don't let pride interfere with the next part of what Jesus wants to reveal to you, because it is a game changer in terms of you beginning to understand how to go from religion to faith.

There is only holy and unholy. Things described as secular are man-made. They refer to an imaginary middle ground between being saved by Jesus and actively participating in devil worship. Things described as holy are aligned with God's character, His nature, His absolute truth. Unholy things are not of God, not of His nature or His absolute truth. Therefore, unholy things are aligned with Satan, the deceiver. God's Word teaches that we are to let Jesus make us holy by letting Him transform our hearts and minds (our ways of thinking) to become more like Him. This is a command of the Lord. So, if God says we are to let Him make us holy, then that means it's possible for us to actually become like Jesus.

Leviticus 11:44–45 (NIV) says, "I am the Lord your God; consecrate yourselves and be holy, because I am holy. Do not make yourselves unclean by any creature that moves along the ground. I am the Lord, who brought you up out of Egypt to be your God; therefore be holy, because I am holy." And in the New Testament, 1 Peter 1:16 (NIV) says, "for it is written: 'Be holy, because I am holy.'" Many non-Christians and Christians alike dwell in a man-made middle ground when it comes to what they believe. They say things like, "I'm not killing people, but I'm not some crazy born-again Christian" or "As long as I'm not hurting other people, this thing is okay. It makes me happy." These are justified wrong thoughts that encourage people to stay on the fence in mediocre Christianity even though staying in the middle conflicts with God's heart.

It is Jesus who gives you permission to enter into God's holy ground. If you stand in the imaginary middle ground, you're standing in unholy ground owned by Satan. If you try to stand in unholiness and dip your toes in holiness, expect that you will be influenced by the one who dwells where you stand. The longer you remain in middle ground, the more you will be influenced by its corrupt foundation. The byproduct of unholiness is justifying and taking up sin, and subsequently, separation from the Lord. As sin justifies itself, it takes on the appearance of virtue and is just accepted without consideration for God's truth. If our conscience is not bothered by a conflict, we can go on as we are without having to address our sin.

God knew this middle-ground thinking would occur. It started even during the ministry of Christ here on earth. God refers to it in Revelation 3:16 (NIV) as "lukewarm": "So, because you are lukewarm—neither hot nor cold—I am about to spit you out of my mouth." Jesus is speaking to the church of Laodicea here. In ancient times, it was customary for people to drink hot or cold beverages at their feasts and in their religious sacrifices, but they never drank a lukewarm beverage. Since Laodicea did not have its own water source, it depended upon the numerous hot springs in the nearby city of Hierapolis, and the connected aqueducts, for water. However, by the time the water reached Laodicea it had cooled to a lukewarm temperature. Lukewarm water is more likely to harbor diseases, therefore, it would need to be cooled or re-heated prior to being fit for consumption. The lukewarm taste of the Laodiceans' religion made Jesus feel so sick He felt like vomiting the church out of His mouth. From Jesus' perspective, those who are "lukewarm" are actually in a worse condition than those who are "cold."

Middle-ground thinking is partially why we see such division in the church on world issues. There are church leaders and members who reside in the middle ground and teach from that perspective, just as there are those who reside in holiness and teach and empower from the perspective of heaven. How does someone begin to understand the difference? It is only by establishing your own personal relationship with Jesus and pursuing His truth that you will develop a solid confidence in who Jesus is and what God says is holy. In knowing His nature, you will begin to identify teaching that falls outside of it.

Jesus has a heart to restore the damage of middle-ground thinking that may have influenced you. In His wisdom and goodness, He wants to help you understand the difference between what is holy and what is unholy, and how to get your feet out of the middle ground and into His holiness.

For those of you who are list-oriented thinkers, this may really speak to your heart. While having a relationship with Jesus is not a check-the-box kind of thing, sometimes we need simple and precise directions for how to move forward and get out of unholiness. In Romans, especially chapters 6–8, God gives us exactly that:

- Stop sinning. Just take a moment to acknowledge that change is hard. Sin behaviors become habits over time. As you pursue Jesus and He reveals your unintentional and intentional sins, He is simultaneously asking you to choose to stop them. In 1 Corinthians 9:27 (NIV), Paul describes the action needed to stop sinning as "strik[ing] a blow to my body," meaning, commanding your flesh to stop doing what is unholy. Confess, repent, and invite Jesus to help you choose holiness. As sin falls off you and righteousness grows, your understanding will increase.

- Don't look back at your life in sin longingly. It is in looking back longingly that new habits fail and where you will more easily succumb to old temptations.

- Don't abuse your freedom in Christ. It is a gift, but it requires your investment. If you want more of Him, you need to give more of yourself.

- You have been released from religion. Therefore, in Christ, stop living in it. Pursue relationship. Seek to learn the difference between religion and faith and how that difference looks in your life. In an authentic relationship with Christ, you are faithful, not religious.

- Let God develop discernment in you. Discernment builds through reading Scripture, prayer, and relationship development with Him. You will begin to see through the lens of heaven as you mature in discernment.

- Let Jesus reveal to you His absolute truth so it can begin to cancel contradictions in your thinking. It may be true that you have sinned, but your truth in Jesus is you're a saint, not a sinner.

- Live adventurously expectant with God, not setting expectations for Him or for what He will do, but expecting He will show up as you walk out one step at a time with Him. Learn to wait upon the Lord in this journey because the waiting brings maturation to your faith.

- God wants to shape your life along the line of Jesus' life. Hope for and pursue this with Him. God's Word says it's possible. The Father longs to return you to the place of holiness He offers you in Christ Jesus.

God established in Romans 4:25 (NIV) that "He was delivered over to death for our sins and was raised to life for our justification." In accepting His promise and saying yes to Jesus as your Savior and the Lord of your life, Jesus should become your litmus test for everything you believe. Everything gets checked against who Jesus is, including what you believe about Him, yourself, other people, politics, education, world events, the economy, the church, your neighbor, etc. Everything you believed before you received Jesus and asked Him to influence your life as the Lord of it is tainted by unholiness. He wants you to see through the lens of heaven on all those subjects. At first, this will be a discipline you'll need to exercise with Him, but it will become a more natural way of relating to Him as you mature in your relationship. You'll find there's not a single situation He doesn't have an opinion about.

Transforming your heart and mind in Christ Jesus is a lifelong journey. Sometimes you'll fail. Jesus is not frustrated with your learning process, your mistakes, or your faith maturity. He just wants you to love the experience so you can receive all He has for you.

Are you confident that you have accepted Jesus as both your Savior and the Lord of your life? If you're not, I want to lead you in a prayer to do that so you can be confident and continue to mature in your relationship with Jesus. Pray with me: "Thank you, Lord Jesus, for saving me by your blood. I confess my sins to you. I confess everything I allowed to interfere with our relationship. I want to be made holy. I ask you to forgive me and to become my Savior and the Lord of my life. I invite you to invade my circumstances, Lord Jesus. I want to receive all you have for me. I want to know you and hear you, and for you to reveal all the contradictions in my life. Help me understand the Father's will for my life. Help me to know how He sees my heart, for the things I thought were hidden are not hidden from you. I invite you to remind me of those things so I can confess and repent and keep nothing hidden from you. I want to be vulnerable with you. I don't want to hold back. Father, your Word says in Matthew 6:14 (NIV), "For if you forgive other people when they sin against you, your heavenly Father will also forgive you." I receive your forgiveness, Father, and I ask you to help me see any places where I have unforgiveness in me. Lead me to resolve those places of unforgiveness with you so I can receive the fullness of what you have for me. Glory be yours, Lord Jesus. I love you. Thank you. In the mighty name of Jesus I pray. Amen."

If you prayed that prayer and meant it, God responded by putting the fullness of His nature within your spirit and your spirit was saved. You are a spirit being that happens to have a soul and is housed in a body (1 Thessalonians 5:23). Your next steps are to walk with Jesus and develop an understanding of all He did for you so that truth can begin to influence your soul and body responses.

CHAPTER 2

Developing a Sensitivity to the Holy Spirit

A few months before we left for Cuba, my sister, along with the pastor who was also leading the trip, had an informational meeting. It was an opportunity for us to learn more about our visas and the details of traveling to a country restricted from the US, and what we would be doing there. After the business of the meeting was completed, the pastor began praying over some of the women who were there. I watched as she spoke powerful prayers using words I didn't know, but could feel the peace of God through them, as well as His assurance that what I was experiencing was real, authentic, and available to me. I was fascinated watching her and seeing the response of women who she knew nothing about as she spoke God's truth to them. I wanted what she had. I wanted more of Him. I wanted to do that kind of thing for God. I had no idea how to get there, but I believed that if I kept saying yes to God, I would.

I kept having dreams during this time of preparation, and a few days after returning home from this meeting, I had another one that knocked my socks off. In the dream, there was a moment where I opened a door at the end of a long hallway. In the room, all the way in a corner, was Satan. He was sitting at a desk, hunched over and sulking, with a cloak covering his head. Next to him was a demon floating and consoling him. When the demon saw me, it screeched and slammed the door in my face. Unlike the first dream, this one did not need interpretation. I knew immediately what God was showing me. I knew that my pursuit of Jesus was bringing me out of my old and into His new. I knew that Satan was sulking over the fact that he had lost permission in my life because I was now being obedient to God, and there was nothing he could do about it. Because I was in Christ Jesus, Satan had no power over me.

When the day came to leave for Cuba, despite all God had been doing, I still had that nagging hesitation bumping up against my heart's desire for more of God. I wrote in my journal, "Come alive in me in a way that I can feel and so that I can know you in a new way. Allow me to be in Your presence and hear your voice." I had no idea why I wrote those things—I'm not sure I really even knew what they meant at the time. So much was not making sense to me, but I wanted more God, so I kept walking forward.

One night, we headed out from Havana to a small home church for a worship service. A thunderstorm roared outside, and just a few minutes into the storm, the electricity went out. This small space, filled with what felt like hundreds of people, was hot, sticky, shoulder to shoulder, standing room only. Despite the lack of physical comforts, this space had something powerful happening within it that captured my awareness, and I wanted to experience it. I wanted to experience what God was doing there. In the dark, the pastor shouted a loud, bold, and powerful word. I observed the multitudes around me having what appeared to be profound personal encounters with the Holy Spirit throughout the service. They were praising and raising hands to

Him—arms above the head, freely raised in a praise position. Some were dancing in whatever room they could find in the aisle, and some were speaking in Spirit tongues. This was my first time seeing and hearing all of this. I had lots of questions.

Throughout my life, this was all stuff I had heard of happening in "Charismatic" churches or in other countries, but I had never been exposed to it. Despite my lack of past experience, I knew just being in this place was going to prompt something of God within me. I hoped, watched, and waited, and…nothing. I kept waiting. Cuban worship services are long. I waited a long time. I wanted God to do something amazing for me. I wanted Him to touch my heart somehow and encounter me, to let me know He saw I was there. As the evening went on with no response, I began to think to myself, "I said yes to go on this mission trip, and I did all the things to get ready for it, and I am standing right here, Lord." I walked out of the service disappointed that God did not do what I hoped He would do in me. I felt like I had been robbed of something I deserved to have. And as I walked onto the bus to leave, I thought, "I heard about what you have done for other women on these trips. I showed up, but you didn't."

I sat on the bus, sulking, when another woman in our group came and sat next to me. I wasn't happy about that. I wanted to sulk alone. It felt good to wallow in self-pity, and I wanted to stay there. But Jesus had other plans, and He met me right where I was and revealed His heart to me through this woman and our conversation.

Before I knew it, I heard the Father say, "You're so deep into control that you're even trying to control your relationship with me."

I had just been made fully aware that God knew about my tendency to control every aspect of my life and that I was not successfully hiding it from Him.

Up to that point, I had been unwilling to have that conversation with the Father because deep down I knew it would mean addressing why I needed to control everything, and I had some serious fear about that. That night during the worship service, my impulse to control set expectations in my mind for how God should meet me. When He didn't do it the way I expected, I was disappointed and upset with Him.

Control was the lord of my life, but Jesus wanted to be in that position. Because of His faithfulness to meet me and reveal this to me, I willingly came into agreement with Him and pressed in for the reasons behind my need for control and His instructions for how to let go of my need for control. I had been in a control mentality for so long, I didn't even know what the opposite of it was. I didn't know about surrender.

In Jesus' gentleness, He revealed I had been believing the lie that I was worthless, insufficient, and inadequate. Fear partnered with control and persuaded me to protect my false sense of insufficiency and inadequacy so no one else would see how insufficient I was. If I could control everything, I could keep my weaknesses to myself. I had been doing this my entire life while fully unaware of it. Every time I came into agreement with a lie about myself, I gave that lie permission to spiral me further and further away from God until I could not even recognize the root lie I was believing.

In that moment on the bus, Jesus was showing me that control is the opposite of His nature. He is in charge of our redemptive process, but He does not control us or our lives. He knows our free will means that some will decide not to love and live for Him, but He was willing to do that in order to walk and talk with us freely. God enforcing control over us conflicts with His allowance of free will.

There is a form of control we do need to engage in as the body of Christ. As a general is also in charge of men, and soldiers are in charge of their weapons, you must keep control of your mind and the thoughts you dwell on, as you are personally responsible for those things. You can't just claim grace and not be active in your faith. Understand the distinction: The only control you have is your choice to pick up your kingdom weapons and press forward as God leads you, rather than being passive in your faith. Don't try to control God, all your circumstances, or other people. Ephesians 1:20–23 (MSG) says, "God raised Him from death and set Him on a throne in deep heaven, in charge of running the universe, everything from galaxies to governments, no name and no power is exempt from His rule. And not just for the time being, but forever. He is in charge of it all and has the final word on everything. At the center of all this, Christ rules the church.... The church is Christ's body, in which He speaks and acts, by which He fills everything with His presence."

Later that night, as a group, we sat and processed what we observed. I shared that I wanted what I had observed, but I didn't know how to get there. The pastor responded with words that have resounded in me since that moment. She said, "We will pray that you experience Holy Spirit, instead of just observe Holy Spirit." With that seemingly simple response, I had an epiphany of significant depth about the difference between observing the things of God and experiencing God. I knew beyond a shadow of a doubt that we are designed to experience everything I had witnessed God doing in others that night but that I had chosen to dwell on the observation deck.

Acts 2:38 (ESV) says, "And Peter said to them, 'Repent and be baptized every one of you in the name of Jesus Christ for the forgiveness of your sins, and you will receive the gift of the Holy Spirit.'" From the observation deck, I had been observing the Holy Spirit work in the lives of others, but I was not experiencing Him because I hadn't invited Him to get into my life and to mature my faith. I hadn't invited Him because I didn't know I needed to. While I had been given the Holy Spirit in the moment I was saved, and He had been dwelling in my spirit, I had never engaged Him and had just assumed He was licensed to do what He wanted in my life. At the same time, I had no idea that He cared about all the details of my life and wanted to be involved.

I also never considered that He honored my free will and wouldn't just start doing things without an invitation. As if that weren't enough, it was a completely new realization for me that my unrepented sin could get in the way of my experience of the Holy Spirit. I didn't know how to confess and repent, so unrepented sin, in the form of the desire to control everything, was chronically interfering. My mind was blown with this revelation. John 16:13

(NIV) says, "But when He, the Spirit of truth, comes, he will guide you into all the truth. He will not speak on his own; he will speak only what he hears, and he will tell you what is yet to come."

In John 14, Jesus tells the disciples He will ask the Father to send the Holy Spirit, the Advocate, the Spirit of truth. The Holy Spirit is the third member of the Trinity only because He is the third member we learn about. His placement in the Trinity is not a representation of the Holy Spirit being less important. We are affirmed of this in John 20:22 (NIV), after Jesus' death and resurrection, when He breathed on the disciples and said, "Receive the Holy Spirit." To truly receive something is to invite it into your life. The disciples needed to invite the Holy Spirit to influence their lives. You also need to invite the Holy Spirit into your life. Once invited, He will begin partnering with the Lord Jesus to bring a revelation of God's desire for the details of your life and empower you to overcome any contradictions or sins that are in the way of you stepping into God's will. When God declares something for your life, you have to be in a posture to hear and receive it if you want to make sense of it. Inviting the Holy Spirit to influence your life is an essential step to avoid missing the call.

Galatians 5:25–26 (MSG) says, "Since this is the kind of life we have chosen, the life of the Spirit, let us make sure that we do not just hold it as an idea in our heads or a sentiment in our hearts, but work out its implications in every detail of our lives. That means we will not compare ourselves with each other as if one of us were better and another worse. We have far more interesting things to do with our lives. Each of us is an original." The Holy Spirit is so important. He deserves our attention. He is the very presence of God living inside those who believe in Jesus. Mediocre Christianity is encouraged by the teaching of a big, vengeful God, a small Jesus, and no Spirit. If we're leaving an entire member of the Trinity out of our faith experience and our life details, we can't expect anything other than mediocrity.

Getting to know the Holy Spirit means also learning about the spirit realm. The Holy Spirit is the only Spirit of God but is not the only spirit. When we acknowledge the Holy Spirit, we simultaneously must acknowledge the opposite spirit, Satan. This subject often ignites intimidation and general discomfort among Christians. In my experience, that intimidation and discomfort is the result of avoidance of the spirit realm. Do we feel discomfort and intimidation because the church avoids the subject, or do we avoid the subject because of the discomfort and intimidation?

By acknowledging Satan, we must acknowledge what God's truth says about him. God did not create Satan as we know him. When God created the world, God said that it was good (Genesis 1:31). This means that even the spirit realm did not have demons at that time. By Genesis chapter three, Satan is present and tempting Eve. Therefore, sometime between God saying His creation was good and chapter three, there was a rebellion in the spirit realm and many angels turned against God to follow Satan. When Satan fell, he took those angels with him, and now they are demons (fallen angels) who serve Satan (Luke 10:18, Revelation 12:7-10).

Many believe the passage in Ezekiel 28:12-17 is a description of the king of Tyre. Others believe it is an account of the fall of Satan. I believe it is both and that God uses this interaction to help us understand what is happening in the spirit realm when we see evil in the natural world. The king of Tyre came into agreement with a demonic entity that then influenced his rebellious behavior. I believe that Ezekiel is speaking to that demonic entity as well as directly to the king. God affirms this through the expressions, "you were in Eden" and "you were on the holy mountain of God." These descriptions would not have applied to the king of Tyre. The passage also states in verse 15 that iniquity was found in him, affirming that God did not create evil.

Satan gets his authority and power from us, it is not given by God. He steals, kills, and destroys, and the more permission we give him to take inroads into our life, the more power and permission we give him to influence. He is the deceiver, the father of lies. All lies come from Satan, and all things from Satan are the opposite of the Spirit of God. All humans, even Christians, have the capacity to believe his lies. Lies are a strategic part of Satan's plan for derailing the church, getting people to worship him (because he loves to be worshiped even if you don't realize what you're doing), and as I shared from my own testimony, he has been successful. Satan enjoys convincing Christians that there is no significance to the Trinity or to knowing God, Jesus, and the Holy Spirit. When Christians believe this lie, they are unintentionally coming into agreement with Satan and giving him permission to continue exercising his power in their life. Avoiding or ignoring the Holy Spirit is literally telling God, the creator of the universe, that the gift He gave you, the fullness of His presence within you, is not enough.

Romans 12:2 (NIV) says, "Do not conform to the pattern of this world, but be transformed by the renewing of your mind. Then you will be able to test and approve what God's will is—His good, pleasing and perfect will." The longer we stay in mediocrity, the more we will conform to the world and its influence. Often, Christians living in mediocrity have some awareness of the presence of God and may even have moments where they feel prompts from the Holy Spirit or hear from God. If that's you, what you're experiencing is either the beckoning of the Holy Spirit from deep within your spirit or the enemy mimicking God to distract you. The Holy Spirit desires an invitation from you and patiently honors your free will until you offer Him that invitation. The Holy Spirit is the plug, the essential source of power that will open the door for you to move into the fullness of all that Jesus desires to be for you and to understand (discern) the things of heaven.

Discernment is taking up God's perspective and exercising the mind of Christ through the activation of the entire Trinity within you. Discernment is a gift from the Lord, and it matures in you over the course of your life. Just like everything else God does, discernment begins in your heart and then renews your ways of thinking.

Colossians 2:8 (NIV) says, "See to it that no one takes you captive through hollow and deceptive philosophy, which depends on human tradition and the elemental spiritual forces of this world rather than on Christ." "Hollow and deceptive philosophy" refers to empty and wrong ways of teaching and thinking that do not align with God's truth. These teachings and thoughts often sound virtuous to those who do not know God's nature, but when viewed through the lens of Christ, are not a representation of God's truth. These thoughts easily come when the Holy Spirit has not been invited.

Ephesians 5:6–7 (MSG) says, "Don't let yourselves get taken in by religious smooth talk. God gets furious with people who are full of religious sales talk but want nothing to do with Him. Don't even hang around people like that." Religion, law, and doctrine are "human tradition." And the "elemental spiritual forces" of this world are the human activities and the demonic spiritual presence that occur on this earth and conflict with God's nature. This spiritual conflict is going on around you all the time, whether you want to acknowledge it or not. You can either show up with "the plug" and all the protection and provision of heaven, or you can show up without them.

The word "demonic" may immediately bring to mind a Hollywood-type portrayal of demonic possession. You may find you're stuck in that kind of thinking, and that may be simply because it's all you've been exposed to. "Demonic" describes everything that is not of God. Sometimes, demonic things represent themselves like a demon in a movie, as in the Mark 9 example of Jesus healing the demon-possessed boy. Most of the time, demonic influences in the world are more subtle, and without developing discernment, Christians can live their entire life having no idea of ways the demonic influences them or their circumstances.

God does not depend on human tradition, but He is a God that honors some tradition. Traditions are not salvation-related issues, and tradition in itself is not evil or wrong, but when we are seeking what honors God and what does not, we must look to the Bible for our traditions, not our pastor, our congregations, or our culture. Take it to God and ask Him, "Does this tradition honor You?" His way is always the opposite of cultural norms and man-made traditions. His ways are higher, and His truth is not to be sacrificed on the altar of public opinion.

Ephesians 4:17–20 (MSG) says, "And so I insist—and God backs me up on this—that there be no going along with the crowd, the empty-headed, mindless crowd. They've refused for so long to deal with God that they've lost touch not only with God but with reality itself. They can't think straight anymore. Feeling no pain, they let themselves go in sexual obsession, addicted to every sort of perversion. That's no life for you. You learned Christ!… Since, then, we do not have the excuse of ignorance, everything—and I do mean everything—connected with that old way of life has to go."

First Corinthians 2:14 (NIV) says, "The person without the Spirit does not accept the things that come from the Spirit of God but considers them foolishness, and cannot understand them because they are discerned only through the Spirit." Christians who are swimming in the stream of cultural norms and blindly accepting things said by the "good people" they agree with are missing out on heavenly discernment. Those the world might identify as "good people" are not always moving in the goodness of God. Someone can demonstrate eloquent, articulate and gentle communication and still have unholy motivations. Learning to discern what represents God's nature and what doesn't is a beautiful gift that comes from the Holy Spirit working in us as we soak in God's truth.

Ephesians 4:30 (MSG) says, "Don't grieve God. Don't break His heart. His Holy Spirit, moving and breathing in you, is the most intimate part of your life, making you fit for Himself. Don't take such a gift for granted." Are you unsure if you have ever invited the Holy Spirit to get involved in the intimate details of your life and to influence your circumstances? He desires for you to be confident in this. If you are ready to take that step with Him, say this simple prayer out loud:

"Father, thank you that I am saved by the blood of Jesus. Thank you that He is the Lord of my life. Thank you that because of His sacrifice, I received your Holy Spirit, who resides within my spirit. I invite you, Holy Spirit, to begin influencing my circumstances and to help me to change my negative habits. Thank you that you empower me into all the things the Father has for me. Help me to understand the fruit of your Spirit within me. Help me to understand the contradictions in my life and to change my old negative habits and thoughts for more of you. Help me to hear your voice and to learn to yield to the Father's will for my life. I surrender my own will to you. I trust you. Amen."

CHAPTER 3

Canceling Fear and Taking Up Authority

As a child, I had a fear that someone was hiding under my bed at night. I would turn on the hall light, then run and jump on my bed, even though it was high enough off the ground that I could see under it. I believed that if I could just make it onto the bed and under the covers, the person waiting under my bed with a knife would choose not to cut my Achilles tendon that night. I did this as if the moment I was getting into the bed was the only option they had to hurt me, and if they missed the chance, they had to wait another day. Turns out, my brother used to hide under my bed and grab my ankles, which is probably one of the sources of this fear. I love you, Mark.

Once I was secure in my protective sheets, I'd lay in bed and yell for my mom or dad to turn off the hall light. Looking back, I can see that none of it made any sense, but because I didn't have truth to bump up against it, a nonsense lie took hold of my thinking and affected me for years until I was willing to really deal with it because, at thirty years old, I was still looking under my bed every night.

As a culture, we have begun to just accept fear as a way of life and tolerate it because so many struggle with it. Our kids are inundated by the spirit of fear, and we often allow the curse of fear to have influence in our children. It's evidenced by irrational acts of fear, like me jumping into my bed. "It's normal to have fear," we say. But since fear is of Satan, the opposite of the nature of God, it's not normal to have fear when we're in Jesus and have the Holy Spirit residing within us. Fear is not normal in the kingdom. It is incompatible with the Trinity. God desires us to develop a fear of the Lord—a reverence for Him and His sovereignty—not to be fearful. If you struggle with fear, it is because somewhere in your life you intentionally or unintentionally came into agreement with fear, and in doing so, gave permission to fear to pursue you. Fear took that permission and has displaced God's nature, the peace of Jesus, within you.

The chains of fear are broken when a reverence for God is established. Fear cannot reside where there is awe and reverence for God. Proverbs 1:7 (NIV) says, "The fear of the Lord is the beginning of knowledge, but fools despise wisdom and instruction." Fearing God is to revere Him in the deepest sense of the word with a posture of awe. It is to love and respect Him so deeply that the idea of displeasing Him feels horrible. It is to honor and respect Him so deeply internally that it is demonstrated outwardly. A proper fear of God develops our faith and increases our heavenly wisdom.

In Ephesians 4:17–24, Paul makes key distinctions that are essential for believers to understand on this side of the cross. They are meant to help guide you as you step out of mediocrity and into an authentic awe and reverence of God. Paul distinguishes between the old self that was crucified with Christ (Romans 6:6) and the new self, made alive in Christ (born again).

In these instructions for Christian living, Paul tells us that we are no longer to live as we did before Jesus (old self), for our hearts were hardened toward God in that place. The more a heart is hardened, the less sensitive and reverent the person is toward God. Living from the old self keeps us in a place where we cannot hear or discern God. Paul goes on to explain that we are to put off our old self (the way we lived before Jesus) and to be made new in the attitude of our minds; and to put on the new self, like God in true righteousness and holiness.

The old self is influenced by all sin and demonic strongholds (the Greek word for stronghold means "prison of deception") that were allowed when we were separated from Christ Jesus (like fear). It desires power, control, comfort, and approval, and is willing to enter into sin in order to accomplish those desires. The old self is performance-driven and rejects the gospel in exchange for self-pleasing activities and beliefs. The old self believes and justifies its own desires to earn their worth, value, and favor with God. Since our fleshly desires are controlled by our needs, our needs become heart idols, the objects of our desire. Jesus is the only antidote for this need for power, control, comfort, and approval.

While in Cuba, one morning the Lord woke me early, before everyone else. Jesus prompted me to go downstairs to have time with Him, so I went. As soon as I began to pray, the Lord blessed me with these words: "Stop trying to control everything. Allow me to bless you."

Then, I audibly heard the soft, loving, and gentle voice of God ask me to get on my knees. In response to the King of the universe who was asking me to do something, I declined.

He asked again. I could hear in His voice that He wanted to bless me and that I needed to be postured on my knees to receive it. But again, I said no. He responded by calling me by name and again lovingly encouraging me, "Emily, get on your knees." This time, I did, and the moment my knees hit the ground, out came all my snot and tears.

Everything was releasing, every unconfessed sin He brought to my mind got confessed, and I received His forgiveness. I prayed and asked for more awareness of His presence in my life. I asked for His grace to overwhelm me. I prayed against the fear and pride in my life that kept me from kneeling the first time He asked. The entire time, I felt Jesus' presence consuming me.

Although it was not easy for me to find willingness to do this with Him, I was grateful for His persistence. What I didn't understand at the time, but do now, is He was being Jesus in skinny jeans for me, showing me the fear, pride, control, and unconfessed sin that were my old self. I was trying to bring them with me into my relationship with Jesus, and He was telling me that there's no room for the things of my old self with Him. They have to stay with the old self, and we have to take up our new self in Christ Jesus. A gentle whisper reminded me of who God is and transformed my heart. We tend to think we need to see God bring fire, wind and waves to demonstrate His love when in actuality, His still small voice is more than sufficient.

James 4:7–10 (MSG) says, "So let God work his will in you. Yell a loud no to the Devil and watch him make himself scarce. Say a quiet yes to God and He'll be there in no time. Quit dabbling in sin. Purify your inner life. Quit playing the field. Hit bottom, and cry your eyes out. The fun and games are over. Get serious, really serious. Get down on your knees before the Master; it's the only way you'll get on your feet."

Jesus killed the old self with Him on the cross. Your old self was too far gone to be fixed, so when you recognized Jesus as your Savior and Lord, He killed it on the cross and gave you a new self to be conformed into His image. In that moment, you were born again. Therefore, don't counsel your old self or try to bring it with you into the new. It's dead on the cross. Don't remodel your old self. It's dead on the cross. Don't listen to the voice of your old self. It's been killed on the cross.

In Ephesians 1–4, Paul is telling the Ephesians who they are in Christ Jesus. He regularly tells them to put on their new self and not resort to their old self. This repetitive language is because habit changing—learning the difference between your old and new self and responding accordingly—takes time and intention. It's a process of cultivating the nature of God, who now resides within you. The only voice your new self is to pay attention to is that of Jesus and the Holy Spirit. They only minister to your new self because they know Jesus killed your old self on the cross. The Trinity is not interested in talking to your old, dead self.

A few days after this moment on my knees with God, a woman approached me after a worship service and indicated she had something to tell me. I grabbed my interpreter and turned on the voice recorder in my phone because I didn't want to forget a single thing she said. For several minutes she spoke God's truth into my heart, but there was one thing she said that hit me hard and marked me for life. "God sees your righteous heart," she said. Hearing this excited and humbled me simultaneously. Immediately, I had a new understanding of who Jesus really is and what it is to have Jesus in my heart. I very suddenly realized that God the Father only sees me through Christ (that is, He only sees my new self).

I was also learning more about how the Lord communicates. The way I felt when He spoke to me a few days before is exactly how I felt at that moment. I felt empowered, calm, encouraged, peaceful, and inspired. The hasty, fearful voice had been silenced. My heart was pierced with this heavenly truth: It doesn't matter what I've done or what's been done to me. When I am in Christ Jesus, the Father only sees my righteous heart. He only sees my potential because the blood of Jesus covers me. He only sees my new self, alive in Christ, not my old self who is dead on the cross.

When He looks at you, He sees you through the lens of Christ. He sees your righteous heart. Have you ever been taught that? This truth conflicts with all the lies from the spirit of fear that say God condemns His sons and daughters. Are you trying to keep your old self alive? If you are, that pattern of behavior is interfering with your relationship with the Lord. He has no interest in fixing what He killed. He wants you to take the new He has given you and step into life with Him. Mediocre Christianity will try to keep you in your old life, in the comfortable dysfunction of being a Christian in name only, but never really experiencing or coming to know Jesus in the new life He died to give you. Don't let it.

The good news is that God has a strategy for you to step into your new life, to be free from fear and all the detrimental things of your old life, and to establish a reverent fear of the Lord within you. He wants to do a divine exchange, and developing an authentic reverence—a holy fear—of the Lord God Almighty is the first step for you to take. The demonic cannot reside in the same space where a true reverence for God has been established.

If you feel overwhelmed looking at your big picture right now, pause for a moment. Just take one small, intentional step at a time and seek Jesus in skinny jeans along the way. Let Him overwhelm you, rather than letting the process overwhelm you.

Fearing God grows your faith. True fear of the Lord will cause you to place your faith and trust for all things in Him alone. In the book of Exodus, fear tried to win over the Israelites as the Egyptians pursued them. In Exodus 14:31 (NIV), God's Word tells us that after the Israelites crossed through the Red Sea on dry ground and saw how God destroyed the Egyptian army, they "feared the Lord and put their trust in Him." In other words, fear pursued them, they chose God, their faith grew as they watched God's majesty on display, and they became a God-fearing people. The same is true today.

Fearing God requires that you recognize all the attributes of God, including His holiness, justice, mercy, and love. Because of His holiness, God cannot be in the presence of sin. He is indignant with righteous anger about sin. In His authority, God has the power to punish those who stand arrogantly against Him and break his commands. I am fully aware that identifying God's holiness and authority is not culturally acceptable language and that many teach Jesus without ever teaching about the holiness of God. But I will not sacrifice truth on the altar of public opinion.

When Christians don't *acknowledge* the fullness of who God is, they cannot experience the fullness of who God is. You're here to get out of that kind of mediocrity, so I'm going to be real about who God is. You cannot truly love God while ignoring any part of who He is. You cannot truly serve God and serve your own will. It's one or the other. They are incompatible. You can exercise your free will and choose to remain in the comfortable dysfunction of mediocrity, or you can choose the opposite by getting uncomfortable and a little vulnerable with God and continuing to pursue Him deeper.

In chapter 4 of the book of Daniel, God gives us a beautiful example of what it is to fear God through Nebuchadnezzar's written memory of how God transformed his heart. Nebuchadnezzar had cultivated and was enjoying his own majestic life. He had a nightmare that triggered fear in him, and in response, he sent for his wise men and dream interpreters: the magicians, enchanters, astrologers, and witches. Not one was able to interpret. That is, until Daniel showed up. Daniel had the Spirit of God within him, and that set him apart from the others. (This is still true today. The Spirit of God is set apart from witches, astrologers, psychics, magicians, etc. They are not of God now just as they were not of God in Daniel's time.)

Daniel received interpretation for Nebuchadnezzar's dream. You can read about it in Daniel 4:20–26. Along with the dream interpretation, Daniel also spoke a warning from the Lord to Nebuchadnezzar to renounce his sins (confess and repent), to do what is right, and to be kind to the oppressed. Daniel spoke to Nebuchadnezzar on behalf of God and promised the king that by coming into alignment with God in these ways, his prosperity would continue.

God was giving Nebuchadnezzar an opportunity to receive truth and transform his life with the Lord. Nebuchadnezzar did not heed the warning and went right on living in arrogance, according to the world's ways, and for his own self-glorification. Verses 28–32 tell us how, twelve months later, what God decreed for King Nebuchadnezzar came to pass and the natural and spiritual consequences of his sin manifested.

King Nebuchadnezzar has a redemption story. He was restored to his throne after the season of consequence from his sin, and chapter 4 closes in verse 36 with this encouragement: "At the same time that my sanity was restored, my honor and splendor were returned to me for the glory of my kingdom. My advisers and nobles sought me out, and I was restored to my throne and became even greater than before. Now I, Nebuchadnezzar, praise and exalt and glorify the King of heaven, because everything He does is right and all his ways are just. And those who walk in pride He is able to humble."

In this word to the king, through Daniel, God was also giving you direction to be applied through your relationship with Jesus. God desires for you to walk with Jesus daily, listening, confessing, repenting, receiving, and letting Him direct your life as you continue to grow in your reverent fear of the Lord. Jesus' heart is to give you an alternative to sin and its natural and spiritual consequences. It's up to you to receive it.

James 4:7 (NIV) says, "Submit yourselves, then, to God. Resist the devil, and he will flee from you." When God asks you to submit to Him, He means to bring your whole, new, born-again self under the lordship of Jesus. Your body, soul (will/emotions/thoughts/intuition), and spirit all need to come into alignment with His nature. Everything that does not line up with the righteousness of Christ within you is a contradiction and cannot remain. As your flesh and your own will revolt against this, you will feel the conflict. Your flesh will not want to submit, especially if you are in agreement with fear or another demonic stronghold.

Submission to God (another truth that is not approved by our culture) is an act of holiness. It's a recognition of His authority and sovereignty. It is a representation of your heart's state toward Him and your desire for more of Him. Submission is the release of control and is demonstrated through your obedience. Submitting to God positions you to exercise the full power and authority of Christ Jesus that is within you.

Jesus was in submission to God, the Father. During His ministry, Jesus said that He gives you authority over all the power of the enemy, and nothing shall harm you (Luke 10:19). When you are in Christ Jesus and in reverence to God, you'll learn how to exercise the power and authority you've been given for His glory. Maturation in that relationship will develop confidence in the authority Christ has delegated to you over all of Satan's power. Picture a police officer putting his hand up as he stands in the middle of a road with traffic. The cars coming at him are moving fast, they're heavy, they have inertia, they have power. Despite their power, the cars stop when the officer puts out his hand. The cars may have power, but the police officer has authority. Authority scares Satan.

Power alone does not, but exercising power by the authority of Christ Jesus stops the power of Satan.

When you assume Jesus' authority over the power of the devil, the devil must obey you. Proverbs 16:6 says that because of the fear of the Lord, the enemy departs from us. Jesus reinforces this teaching in His ministry in John 14:12 (NIV): "Very truly I tell you, whoever believes in me will do the works I have been doing, and they will do even greater things than these, because I am going to the Father."

As we witnessed in Daniel, authority empowers (gives someone the authority or power to do something), it edifies (instructs or improves someone morally or intellectually), and admonishes (expresses warning or disapproval in a gentle, earnest manner). Authority is always how the Holy Spirit prompts, guides, and represents the Father.

Will you let Jesus complete the divine exchange of all the negative for His positive in Christ Jesus? If you're ready, join me in this prayer: "Father, I come to you because of the blood Jesus shed for me on the cross. Thank you, Jesus. I confess that I have come into agreement with fear, control, and other demonic lies that I now see are not your ways. I repent from those ways and ask you to forgive me. I want to live in submission to you Jesus, my King. I exercise the authority of Christ Jesus that you have given me and right now, in the name of Jesus Christ my Lord and Savior, I proclaim that fear, control, and everything attached to them have no more permission in my life, in my family, and in all future generations. I cancel all of evil's permission to my family line, all of the ways Satan has influenced me, and all of his plans for me, in the name of Jesus Christ. I bind you in Jesus' name and rebuke you. I send you to the feet of my Lord, Jesus. He will deal with you. You may never return. I receive your freedom, Lord Jesus. Help me to reside in your peace and to change my habits. I invite you to do a divine exchange within me, Jesus, and fill those spaces that just opened in me with more of you. Help me to choose your truth and to remain confident in what you've just done for me. I trust you, Father. I trust you, Jesus. Holy Spirit, I trust you to lead me in alignment with the Father's will for me. Thank you. I praise you, Lord. Amen."

CHAPTER 4:

Pursuing the Fruit of the Spirit: Love, Kindness, Joy, and Peace

When God looks at you, this is how He sees you: "But you are a chosen people, a royal priesthood, a holy nation, God's special possession, that you may declare the praises of Him who called you out of darkness into his wonderful light" (1 Peter 2:9, NIV). When you came to Christ Jesus by faith and Jesus came into you, God also sent the Spirit of truth, His Holy Spirit. The fullness of who God is dwells in you. He did not just send a portion of Himself, He sent the fullness of Himself so you would have everything you need to mature into what He sees when He looks at you: your potential in Christ Jesus to face every circumstance from the victory already won.

Ephesians 4:14–16 (MSG) says, "God wants us to grow up, to know the whole truth and tell it in love—like Christ in everything. We take our lead from Christ, who is the source of everything we do. He keeps us in step with each other. His very breath and blood flow through us, nourishing us so that we will grow up healthy in God, robust in love." When we are in relationship with Christ Jesus, we have a promise for God's presence to influence every single one of our circumstances, in the same measure of God that Jesus has, to help us endure any affliction that comes.

Galatians 5:22–23 (NIV) says, "But the fruit of the Spirit is love, joy, peace, forbearance, kindness, goodness, faithfulness, gentleness and self-control. Against such things there is no law." The fruit of the Spirit is synonymous with God's nature. It is who He is. If we're honest, most Christians will say they do not dwell in the fruit of the Spirit within them. We like to visit love, joy, peace, patience, kindness, gentleness, goodness, faithfulness, and self-control. We want to experience all of those virtues more often, but our perspective of the work required to come to the place where we dwell in the nature of the Lord instead of visiting can feel intimidating and overwhelming.

Often, we respond negatively toward this invitation because we would rather choose the things of self. So, if we yield to the flesh instead of the Holy Spirit prompting our spirit, we remain visitors in God's nature while His fullness is dwelling in us waiting for us to say yes to more of Him. God put His nature in us, and He is in charge, but He does not control. He will not force His nature upon us. We must exercise our free will and choose to do the internal work with God that is necessary to cultivate what He has given us.

Jesus has given you a heavenly strategy for how to cultivate the fruit of the Spirit. Rather than being overwhelmed by your emotions and the external circumstances, or the chaos of the world, be overwhelmed by the fact that the Lord God Almighty dwells in you. Are you missing out on that kind of experience with Him? Sometimes, we need to look back to the beginning to understand why we haven't cultivated more fruit in our life to see what has robbed us of God's fruit. In doing so, Jesus restores what He reveals is missing.

In John 14, Jesus encourages the disciples, telling them to believe what they have seen: the work of the Father who is in Jesus. It's an invitation He is extending to believe the great things Jesus has done because of the Father within Him and the intimacy of relationship between Jesus and the Father. In John 14:7 (NIV), Jesus says, "If you really know me, you will know my Father as well."

Knowing Jesus intimately, rather than just knowing about Him, is an invitation to understand why Jesus took religion to the cross and exchanged it for relationship.

It's an invitation to come to know more of the nature of God. Jesus reinforces this in John 15:5 (MSG): "I am the Vine, you are the branches. When you're joined with me and I with you, the relation intimate and organic, the harvest is sure to be abundant. Separated, you can't produce a thing."

Paraphrasing a prophetic message I once heard from Graham Cooke: "God has such affection for you. John 14:23 (NIV): 'Jesus says, "Anyone who loves me will obey my teaching. My Father will love them, and we will come to them and make our home with them."'" Can you hear the affection Jesus has for you in that word? If you love Him, you'll keep His commandments, and you'll come to know how much He delights in you. You'll know how much He is in love with you. Cultivating the fruit of the Spirit put within you by the Holy Spirit is motivated by being so overwhelmed by the love of God that you choose to do the things He stirs in you. The fruit of the Spirit is God's constant nature toward you.

Have you heard the song, "Good Mood" by Richlin? The chorus of the song is the perfect expression of God's heart toward you. God is always joyful toward you. When you explore the fruit of the Spirit in your life circumstances, letting God cultivate them, you'll come to a place where you understand the depth of this truth.

People get turned off when Christians operate outside of the nature of God within them. Maybe you were taught some wrong things about God, but as you mature and learn the contradictions between what you once perceived and who He really is, you have the opportunity to let Jesus transform you. If you desire to call people higher, you need to be letting Jesus transform you and letting the Holy Spirit cultivate His fruit in you, so it is God's true nature that people see in you.

God has given a heavenly strategy for believers to more authentically represent God's heart. The initial experience of being filled with the Holy Spirit was never meant to be a one-time event with Him. Scripture exhorts you to seek daily infilling of the Holy Spirit as part of your intimate relationship. First John 1:7 (NIV) says, "But if we walk in the light, as He is in the light, we have fellowship with one another, and the blood of Jesus, His Son, purifies us from all sin." Remaining in right relationship with Jesus, walking in the light with Him, is necessary if we desire to receive a daily infilling of Holy Spirit. Confessing, repenting and seeking His heart for every circumstance returns us to the fullness of His light. Just as Jesus received the Holy Spirit from a position of right relationship with the Father (see Matthew 3:16), we receive the Holy Spirit from the same position. Ephesians 5:18 (NIV) says, "Do not get drunk on wine, which leads to debauchery. Instead, be filled with the Spirit." In the Greek text, the word for "be filled" is in the continuous present tense, giving the verse the meaning, "Be continuously filled with the fullness of the Holy Spirit."

After Jesus' death and resurrection, Acts 2 tells us, "When the Feast of Pentecost came, they were all together in one place. Without warning there was a sound like a strong wind, gale force—no one could tell where it came from. It filled the whole building." Have you ever been in gale force winds? I haven't, but years ago I took my kids to an experiential museum, and they had a wind tunnel. Gale force winds in nature can get up to eighty-two miles per hour, but the wind tunnel produced sixty-miles-per-hour winds. We were in an enclosed space and a controlled environment, totally safe and protected, but feeling the power of that wind was bonkers and scary. I kept waiting for my legs to get swept up by the wind, and the longer it went on, the tighter I held on to the support bar and my kids.

"Then, like a wildfire, the Holy Spirit spread through their ranks, and they started speaking in a number of different languages as the Spirit prompted them."

The significance of why the Jews were in Jerusalem at the time influenced what God was doing here. They were there for the Feast of Pentecost, a time of thanksgiving for the wheat harvest.

The day of Pentecost was later associated with a remembrance of the Law given by God to Moses on Mount Sinai because the Jews believe that Pentecost is the exact day that Moses went up into Mt. Sinai with God and received the Ten Commandments. They use this time to reflect on being taken out of one season of slavery, being brought into a season of flourishing, and how God gave them the directions for how they were to encounter Him.

It was not a time just about the harvest, it was a time when tens of thousands of people and religious leaders from various regions would congregate in Jerusalem, bringing the fruits of their labor and hoping for the direction and promises of God in the next season.

From the crowd they begin to hear the rustle of voices. They realize that rustle is in their own native tongue, and they wonder who is speaking it. Verses 5–11 describe the bewildered, shocked, and utterly amazed Jews. Jesus' disciples are speaking in their language and declaring what verse 11 (NIV) refers to as the "wonders of God." They couldn't figure out what was going on.

In verse 12 (NIV), they ask, "What does this mean?" and some joke and claim the disciples were drunk on wine. At that moment, Peter stands up and speaks with what scripture describes as "bold urgency" (verses 14–21 MSG). He raises his voice and addresses the crowd, saying, "Let me explain this to you; listen carefully to what I say." Peter begins to describe to them what is taking place before their very eyes. He references the prophet Joel and all he prophesied about the pouring out of the Holy Spirit. He goes on to tell them that this is the moment that they have been waiting for their whole lives. This is the moment of God coming to earth.

Peter then draws their thinking back to David and all he prophesied, starting at verse 29 (MSG). He reminds them of David's faithfulness and of God's promise that the descendants of David would rule His kingdom. He reminds them of how David spoke prophetically about the resurrection of the Messiah, that they would witness it, and that the Father would pour out His Spirit. He goes on to tell them, "This is what you see and hear." He is saying these things to correct any wrong thoughts that are dwelling in the minds of the Jewish leaders, drawing them back to thinking about what it means in alignment with what God has already said.

Can you imagine the environment? They're waiting, seeking God, and praying. Then God's presence falls upon them, crazy stuff begins to happen, and they start asking themselves what all of this means. They just needed to recall what happened on Mount Sinai when Moses received the Ten Commandments. Scripture tells us that a mighty rushing wind came when God came down to Mount Sinai. God chose to go from His realm of heaven and enter into the realm of humanity, showing up as a mighty rushing wind.

What does it mean? That's the question we all should be asking. It's the question the Holy Spirit prompted in their hearts. Why on earth did this fire fall on them, why did they get a supernatural ability to speak a new language, and why were they proclaiming the wondrous works of God in that language? Why was this all happening in a moment when people were waiting for God to do something new? What does it mean? God was choosing to enter into the hopes and passions of the world, and He was saying to them, "In order for the world to experience you as my witnesses, you need to declare the goodness of me to the world. So, I am going to take my Spirit, reveal my glory, and give you words you have no idea how to speak." It was a declaration that God has shown up and He cannot be stopped.

Peter answers the deep question they had, saying, "God is on the move and this is the day you have been waiting for, this is the day of the Lord." He knows that if the Jews hear that the day of the Lord had come and they missed it, it will ruin them. Peter is bold in telling them that they did miss it. He's not letting them off the hook. He goes on to explain about Jesus, who did all these incredible works. Jesus was handed over as part of God's deliberate plan, and they put Him to death. But God raised Him, freeing Him from the burden of death.

Peter traps his audience by drawing them in and then dropping the hammer on them so they understand what this means. He tells them that the day of the Lord has come and they missed it because even though Jesus proved time and time again about the signs and wonders of God, when He was given to you, you killed Him.

Peter holds nothing back as he talks about what happened to Jesus. What he says could be perceived as offensive, yet they are not offended. Peter is upset and hurt, and simultaneously, he tenderly calls out to them and demonstrates what they did in killing Jesus.

Scripture tells us in verse 37 (ESV) that this bold response by Peter "cut to the heart." And that cut to the heart brings about another question: "Brothers, what shall we do?" This question is the demonstration of the loving conviction of the Holy Spirit that Peter's communication prompted. Peter responds to their question by telling them to get out of this sick and stupid culture and change their lives. He urges them to turn to God and be baptized in the name of Jesus Christ, to be forgiven of their sins, and to receive the gift of the Holy Spirit.

Do you feel the power of what's being said? The words of Peter demonstrate the weight of the incredible goodness of what Jesus did for us. Some may read this and think, "I didn't kill Jesus." Some may try to distance themselves from this truth by not wanting to affiliate themselves with bad things other people have done. The reality, though, is that if we live every day as if He doesn't exist in the abundance of who He actually is, then if we lived in His time, we would have been part of the people who murdered Him.

That reality should rip our hearts open. It should also be enough to call us into deeper faithfulness to Him and into a willingness to receive the empowering of the Holy Spirit. The Holy Spirit coming to the upper room is amazing, but the richness of this passage is that life is being offered. God's presence is being offered to us, and He is asking us to take it.

There is much that tries to rob you of the fruit of the Spirit. When we receive Jesus as our Savior and Lord, God also gives us the fullness of His nature. When you choose His nature rather than your old nature, and let it cultivate, His fruit always displaces the negatives. Worry, fear, anxiety, doubt—they are incompatible with the nature of God. If you begin to think about cultivating the fruit of the Spirit as a pleasure, rather than a discipline, you'll also begin to see it as God's provision for you.

Before we mature in faith and knowledge, we may not realize that God is using our experiences to cultivate His fruit within us. I certainly did not understand that early on. But the power of our testimony in Christ Jesus is that as we mature, we can look back and see how He provided for us in ways we didn't know we needed.

The Fruits of Love and Kindness

I began to really understand what Jesus' love and kindness looked like, and how they partner together, several months after I returned home from one of many trips I was blessed to take to Cuba. It played out in such a powerful way that I still often remind myself of it as I reflect on His faithfulness in my life.

Through a process of prayer, Jesus revealed that I had been sulking in self-pity about my friendships. I was longing for real, authentic friendships, but instead of taking it to the Lord to seek His heart, I chose to sulk because I didn't have what I desired. After a few days, I let Jesus grab ahold of my heart on this issue, confessed, repented, and asked Him to help me see my situation as He saw it.

I was already sensing conflict in my relationships. With every step of maturity in my relationship with Christ, there was a revelation in my spirit about the contradiction between where God was taking me and where I was investing my time and energy. I had not yet surrendered my relationships to Jesus. I had just been hoping, or assuming, that my relationships would mature along with where God was taking me. My flesh wanted both spiritual maturation and my relationships, but my spirit was hearing the Holy Spirit beckon me to put the Father, myself, and my family first.

For several weeks I pursued Jesus on this subject, and through that pursuit, I tried to listen and learn, and I certainly made lots of mistakes along the way. But as I dealt with Him about those mistakes, He revealed to me that I had been idolizing my relationships.

Relationships, even superficial ones, had become so important in my life that I positioned them over God, myself, or my family, and therefore compromised what He desired for me. After confessing and repenting my idolatry, I began asking God what I needed to do. One morning in my quiet time, I felt Him prompt me to just have a conversation with the friend with whom I was feeling the biggest tension in this area. I felt He was prompting me to share the radical changes that Jesus was making in me, to acknowledge and apologize for idolizing our relationship, and to share my desire for real and authentic relationship. I sensed deep down that this conversation could quite possibly bring the end of the relationship, and it did.

The next morning, as I began my quiet time, I immediately began weeping, fell to my knees, and asked the Father, "Why did I have to lose the friendship?" You see, not only did I lose that one friendship, but without any conversation, I also lost every relationship within that same friend group.

Immediately upon asking the Lord why, my heart was lifted. In the blink of an eye, the Holy Spirit showed me why the relationship(s) needed to end. I saw two timelines of my daughter's future. One where I stayed where I was, in superficial and idolized relationships and where she spent her life struggling with her identity in Christ and always trying to be who she thought others wanted her to be. This path looked exactly like my life, and I immediately knew I did not want that for my girl.

The second timeline was one where I obeyed and abided where God just put me, and my girl established confidence in who Jesus says she is and lived life from that place of confidence in the righteousness of

Christ and in the favor of God. I went from weeping with sadness to joyful celebration for what He did! That singular moment was the first time I understood His kindness on display in my life.

> **Although it hurt, and had tons of emotion attached to it, in His faithfulness, He kindly and lovingly took me out of what was holding me back so I could experience what He had for me.**

I understood in that moment that His love was being displayed in the revelation that my sin (idolatry) had interfered with my experience of this kind of love and kindness. I also understood that my sin was setting my daughter up to struggle with the same things I struggled with, but my confession and repentance and obedience to God was changing all that. The negative cycle was breaking.

In His love for me, He showed me His kindness, placed me in alignment with Him, and gave me a promise that my daughter, who I did not realize was following the same path, would also come into alignment with Him. That was worth losing everything I thought was important to me. That was worth the pain, emotion, and subsequent two years without friendships as God developed and restored the relationships that matter to Him—with Him, my husband, and my family.

Ephesians 5:1–2 (MSG) says, "Watch what God does, and then you do it, like children who learn proper behavior from their parents. Mostly what God does is love you. Keep company with Him and learn a life of love. Observe how Christ loved us. His love was not cautious but extravagant. He didn't love in order to get something from us but to give everything of Himself to us. Love like that." When I was in Cuba, I felt the Holy Spirit prompting in me that I had potential to be a different woman, mother, Christian, and person. I wanted what I felt He was revealing to me more than I wanted where I was, so I pressed in. The more I pressed into Him, the more I understood that genuine love is shown through a heart of kindness.

Kindness, like all other fruit of the Spirit, grows from a foundation of Jesus' love. In Christ, we are conceived in love. Speaking truth in love to others is our response to how the Holy Spirit empowers us. As I shared in my testimony, as we grow up into all things Jesus, we begin to desire that the people around us will also grow up into all things Jesus. Everything we say to people should represent the fruit of the Spirit—God's nature—and inspire them in their relationship with the Lord Jesus. Learning how to speak God's truth from the place of Jesus' love is how we get to partner with Jesus to help others mature in their faith.

His promise to us in Isaiah 49:15 (NIV), "Can a mother forget the baby at her breast and have no compassion for the child she has borne? Though she may forget, I will not forget you," reminds us that He is loving, kind, and true to us even when we are far away from Him. I was far away from Him in my idolatry, but when I prayed and surrendered that sin and my self-pity, and invited Him to make me satisfied, He responded.

Like Jesus, we can press into the nature of God for His glory and for His outcomes. Before enduring the cross, Jesus ministered to the hearts of those He encountered both directly and indirectly. Directly, for example, at the Sermon on the Mount. Indirectly, through His demonstration of God's nature. We see an example of this in John 13 as Jesus demonstrates the kindness of God, in love, by submitting with humility.

Jesus would be crucified soon, and He knew it. "Having loved His own who were in the world, He loved them to the end" (John 13:1 NIV). Judas had already been prompted by Satan to betray Jesus. "Jesus knew that the Father had put all things under his power, and that He had come from God and was returning to God" (verse 3 NIV). In response, Jesus got up from the meal and assumed the posture of servant, the lowest societal position. He poured water into a basin and began to wash the feet of the disciples. In kindness, humility, and submission to the Lord God Almighty, He came to Judas, the one who was about to betray Him, and washed his feet too. When He came to Simon Peter, the one who was about to deny Him, He not only washed his feet, but when Simon Peter first declined, Jesus waited, persisted, and then washed his feet. Jesus would not let Simon Peter miss this blessing even though He knew he was going to deny Him.

Is there someone who has betrayed or offended you? Maybe you even feel like God has betrayed or offended you. Do the actions of Jesus in John 13 represent someone who would betray, or rather, someone who would love you through the process of understanding the real source of negativity in your life? When we choose to follow Jesus and take up kindness in love, submitting to one another in love and humility (even toward those we disagree with or who betray us), we are demonstrating genuine love, the love of Jesus, the nature of God.

In the next scene of John 13, Jesus admonishes the disciples. To admonish is to exercise authoritative counsel or warning. Since Jesus is the authority, He was demonstrating to the disciples how to exercise authority in love and kindness so they would understand how to exercise godly authority after He was no longer with them in flesh. The purpose of admonition is always to develop the identity of the believer in Christ Jesus. Admonition must be compatible with the good news of the gospel, rooted in God's nature and Jesus' love and kindness, and will always have encouragement for a spiritual increase in Christ attached to it. Romans 2:4 (MSG) says, "In kindness He takes us firmly by the hand and leads us into radical life-change." And 2 Timothy 2:13 (NIV) reassures us that "If we are faithless, He remains faithful, for He cannot disown himself."

The Fruit of Joy

Hebrews 12:2 (NIV) says, "…fixing our eyes on Jesus, the pioneer and perfecter of faith. For the joy set before Him He endured the cross, scorning its shame, and sat down at the right hand of the throne of God." Jesus made it through the worst because of joy. He endured the cross by connecting to His kingdom purpose and the Father's promises, and that carried Him through His circumstances and into a place of rest next to the Father. He counted everything about the cross joy because He was committed to the Father's plan. The same measure of joy that was within Jesus is within you. If Jesus was committed to the Father's plan and counted everything along the way as joy, and you are being made in His image, then you are also learning to commit to the Father's plan and counting all your negative circumstances as joy. Easier said than done, for both Jesus and us.

Do you recall the joy of your salvation? The psalmist, in Psalms 51:12 (NIV) says, "Restore to me the joy of your salvation and grant me a willing spirit, to sustain me." The joy of your salvation is aligned with your pursuit of an intimate relationship with the Lord.

Nehemiah 8:10 (NIV) says, "The joy of the Lord is your strength." Joy comes from knowing who God will be for you no matter your circumstances. If you're feeling weak, don't try to be strong on your own. Rather, accept that joy is God's provision for you because joy is who He is. Have you invested in your relationship with Him? Intimacy with God will cultivate joy.

> **Happiness is a circumstantial and temporary emotion. Joy is designed to be where we live.**

If we rely on the joy of the Lord as our strength, we can be joyful no matter what we face as the nature of God displaces the negatives. The little things in life are really not worth getting upset about. I realized on my last Cuba trip that I spent my lifetime letting the little things set me off, creating anger and offense. God doesn't want us to live that way because it is the opposite of the joy of His kingdom. He wants us to live joyfully, letting things roll off our backs and putting others before ourselves.

In Philippians 4:4 (NIV), we are commanded to "Rejoice in the Lord always. I will say it again: Rejoice!" If God's Word says to rejoice always, that means it is possible. Since God is always joyful, rejoicing with Him ignites an experience of His joy. In other words, rejoicing is your response to experiencing Him.

In John 16:24 (NIV), Jesus says, "Until now you have not asked for anything in my name. Ask and you will receive, and your joy will be complete." Answered prayer cultivates joy within us. If you don't pray, you won't have answered prayers. Are you making time to pray?

Once I was asked to speak at a women's event on the subject of joy. I was affirmed this was an assignment God had for me, so I went back to Him and asked if there was anything more He wanted to teach me about joy before I taught others on the subject. He took me on a journey over a few weeks of recognizing something about myself that was inhibiting my joy.

One day during this process, I walked into my home at the end of the day and stood in the place where I always set my things down. I heard the Holy Spirit say, "You reserve your joy here." My first reaction was, "Wait, what?" but then I immediately understood what He was saying. I had been making a subconscious choice to be an expression of joy all day at my boutique, but to withhold that same joy from my family when I got home at night. I wasn't willfully doing this, but once the Holy Spirit revealed it to me, I knew I needed to confess, repent, and begin to exercise new habits. So I did, immediately. As soon as I finished praying, I felt the flaming arrows of the enemy come. He tried to persuade me that I was not an authentic Christian because of this sin, when in truth, my authenticity was demonstrated by my confession, repentance, and invitation to the Holy Spirit to get into the mix. God showed me those arrows for what they were, took authority over them in Jesus' name, and ended it right there.

I asked the Holy Spirit what else I needed to do to affirm all He had revealed, and I heard Him prompt, "Confess to your husband." So I did. I told him what the Holy Spirit revealed, and I apologized for withholding joy from him and how that affected him and our relationship. I committed to keep working with the Lord so joy could be restored wherever it was broken. He accepted my apology, and within twenty-four hours, the atmosphere in our home, and between us, was completely different. Joy had been restored where I didn't even realize it needed to be.

One day our final destination will be not only entering into *heaven* but entering into joy! Matthew 25:21 (NKJV) says, "Well done, good and faithful servant; you were faithful over a few things, I will make you ruler over many things. Enter into the joy of your lord." Don't miss this opportunity to cultivate joy and experience earth as it is in heaven.

The Fruit of Peace

Peace is a popular word. It is used all the time to represent the absence of war or conflict, it refers to rest, and is even used to fill space without much meaning at all. The *Merriam-Webster Dictionary* defines peace as "a state of tranquility or quiet," such as when describing a place as peaceful or saying your mind is at peace. God's peace is more than just the absence of conflict or a state of rest. It means completeness or wholeness, and it points to the presence of something else.

The Hebrew word translated as peace is shalom, and according to *Strong's Concordance*, it means completeness, soundness, and welfare. Peace in the New Testament is from the Greek word *eiréné*. According to Strong's Concordance, *eiréné* means one, peace, quietness, and rest. It originates from the root word *eirō*, which means to join or tie together into a whole. Therefore, *eiréné* comes from an idea of unity.

The peace of God is more than just the absence of conflict; it is taking action to restore a broken situation. It's more than a state of inner tranquility; it's a state of wholeness and completeness in unity with the Lord.

What is peace? Peace is mentioned 420 times in Scripture. Through His word, God teaches us more and more about the depth of His peace that we can pursue.

Isaiah 32:17 (NIV): "The fruit of that righteousness will be peace; its effect will be quietness and confidence forever."

Isaiah 53:5 (NIV): "But He was pierced for our transgressions, He was crushed for our iniquities; the punishment that brought us peace was on Him, and by His wounds we are healed."

Jesus is peace. He gave us Himself, He gave us peace, and it is designed to perfect us, represent our trust in Him, and help us overcome. Peace cancels fear, trouble, anxiety, worry, doubt, frustration, lies, and second guessing. Peace transcends our natural understanding, and when we surrender to it, peace guards our hearts and minds.

In John 14:27 (NIV), Jesus says, "Peace I leave with you; my peace I give you. I do not give to you as the world gives. Do not let your hearts be troubled and do not be afraid." If we believe what Jesus said in this verse, we need not be asking Him for peace, but rather asking Him to help us cultivate a greater understanding of His peace within us. As the church, we need to change our lenses and start seeing situations where we feel like we need peace as situations where God has appointed an opportunity for us to exercise the peace He has already given us. Therefore, we just need to choose it and exercise it. Our measure of peace increases when we do this, and His peace is then a little bit more established in us for the next circumstance we face where we feel like we need peace.

Isaiah 26:3 (NIV) says, "You will keep in perfect peace those whose minds are steadfast, because they trust in you." When we keep our hearts and minds focused on God in our circumstances, exercising His peace within, peace will eventually become our default response. It won't matter what the outcome is. If we know we are in the center of God's will for us, we will be sure-footed on our foundation despite the terrain. If we come out of His will and do our own thing, we can feel a loss of peace.

Can you think of a situation in your life where you don't have peace? Are you in hot pursuit after the Lord about it? Are you moving in responsive obedience? Peace and disobedience are incompatible. Sometimes God will take our peace if we're not pursuing Him about a circumstance. He may want you to take it to Him in prayer so He can show you what He thinks about it. God's Word says to take every situation to Him in prayer, and when we do, we will encounter His peace.

To really understand peace, we also need to understand the opposites, the emotions and experiences like anxiety and worry, that are incompatible with peace. Thankfulness restores peace and is the antidote to its opposites. Philippians 4:6–7 (NIV) says, "Do not be anxious about anything but in every situation, by prayer and petition, with thanksgiving, present your requests to God. And the peace of God which transcends all understanding, will guard your hearts and our minds in Christ Jesus."

If you're not dwelling in peace, start talking to God about every situation in your life: your family, marriage, children, education, future, career, economy, where you spend your time, who you spend your time with, the books you read—everything. When God's Word says "every situation," He means every situation. Not just the ones that the world would say are a big deal. He wants to be involved in the details of your life, and inviting Him is essential to cultivating His peace within. "For God is not a God of disorder but of peace" (1 Corinthians 14:33, NIV).

Peace protects us from disorder. Chaos is incompatible with peace. When the world is in chaos, we can dwell in peace, standing in the breath of God, aware of the disorder but not in it. We truly can stand firm in the eye of the storm, not yielding to our emotions, and not entertaining "what if" scenarios, but confident in the Holy Spirit and the peace of Jesus that overwhelms us. Psalm 4:8 (NIV) says, "In peace I will lie down and sleep, for you alone, Lord, make me dwell in safety."

Proverbs 14:30 (NIV) says, "A heart at peace gives life to the body, but envy rots the bones." Peace brings abundant life, in the body and in the spirit. Envy robs us of that peaceful abundance. Envy motivates us to strive for something outside of God's desires for us. This striving takes us out of God's desires for us and leaves us not only striving for a lifetime but also without peace.

God knows what you need. He is being very intentional in your current circumstances. Let Him use your circumstances to cultivate His peace within you. Don't miss the lesson. Missing the lesson means repeating the lesson and going longer without peace. We cannot skip past God's lessons. Dive in and receive the fullness of His peace.

Prayer: "Jesus, thank you for your blood that was shed so that I could be saved, receive the Holy Spirit, and come into the presence of God the Father. I am so grateful for what you did for me. Father, I no longer desire to diminish what you have given me. I want to know more about your nature, the fruit of your Spirit. I long for you to cultivate your nature within me and that it would influence my emotions, thoughts, decisions, and behaviors. I want to respond from a place of your Spirit rather than react in emotion and old habits. Holy Spirit, will you help me change my habits, and my muscle memory, so I can learn to dwell in the Father's nature? Than you for hearing my prayer. I trust you will respond. Help me not to miss what you desire to show me. I love you. Amen."

Chapter 5:

Still Pursuing the Fruit of the Spirit: Patience, Faithfulness, Goodness, Self-Control, and Gentleness

The Fruit of Patience

Psalm 5:1–3 (MSG) says, "Listen, God! Please, pay attention! Can you make sense of these ramblings, my groans and cries? King-God, I need your help. Every morning you'll hear me at it again. Every morning I lay out the pieces of my life on your altar and watch for fire to descend." You are increased in the waiting. Between the asking and the receiving is the place of increase where God is developing what will be harvested in your life.

In the Bible, the word patience, *hupomone* in Hebrew, implies "cheerful endurance, steadfastness, constancy or waiting." It is understood as the determination of a person's will, to not be swerved from their deliberate purpose, and their loyalty to faith by even the greatest sufferings. Just like all other fruit of the Spirit, you already have the same measure of patience within you that Jesus has. Exercising godly patience is an outward representation of the strengthening of your relationship with God.

If we're honest, we'd rather not have difficult circumstances. We cannot wait for things to "settle down" or "get back to normal." Do you allow difficult circumstances to affect you in such a way that they interfere with your affect, language, the tone of your voice, or your sleep cycles? Do you give your circumstances permission to interfere with your thought processes and behaviors? The more we give permission to that interference, the more we begin to justify impatient behaviors and other actions that are outside of the fruit of the Spirit. All of this is rooted in looking at difficult circumstances as if they are a heavy problem that you don't want.

When God looks at your circumstances, He sees a divine opportunity to do something miraculous. You can perceive your circumstances in the same way He does if you let His nature flood your thinking and invite Him to divinely exchange the negatives of your difficult circumstances for His miracles. Proverbs 14:29–33 (NIV) says, "Whoever is patient has great understanding, but one who is quick-tempered displays folly. A heart at peace gives life to the body, but envy rots the bones. Whoever oppresses the poor shows contempt for their Maker, but whoever is kind to the needy honors God. When calamity comes, the wicked are brought down, but even in death the righteous seek refuge in God. Wisdom reposes in the heart of the discerning and even among fools she lets herself be known."

On an average day where everything seems to be going your way, you likely have no problem exercising patience. But if you're honest, in difficult circumstances, patience is harder to remember. Adversity isn't to be perceived as a difficult circumstance or a time to surrender the fullness of God within us.

In Christ, adversity is to be seen as the place where God is moving in our life with His sovereign purposes for our spiritual maturation. Adversity is where you exercise and cultivate the fruit of the Spirit.

There was a season in my life when God assigned me to a responsibility that brought adversity. It was a daily, hourly, minute-by-minute practice of surrender, seeking and exercising the fruit of the Spirit to get through that year. I messed up a few times, and He faithfully reminded me to love the learning. The learning required patience. There were moments of impatience when I would ask God to take me out of the circumstance early. Without fail, in just a matter of seconds, the Holy Spirit would convict me and lovingly remind me this was a "salvation assignment" God had chosen me for. After this reminder, my heart would again soften toward God, and I would repent and ask Him to keep using me for His glory. The intensity of the affliction was at times so overwhelming that there were a few days I'd find myself more than once saying, "Lord, when are you going to take me out of this?"

Rewinding a bit, several years prior to this, I had asked God to help me see and quickly stop my wrong thoughts, frustrations, and behaviors that spiraled me out of dwelling in His fruit. I desired that the choices that used to spiral me into negativity for months, weeks, or days at a time could be caught within a matter of seconds or minutes. He faithfully answered this prayer and no longer do those wrong ways of thinking get to affect me for extended periods of time. In our humanness, we will experience the emotions and desires of the flesh. But God has given us a strategy for how to protect ourselves from falling into their trap.

God wants you to strengthen your patient heart now, so when adversity does come, you can exercise His patience as you face it. James 5:7–8 (NIV) says, "Be patient, then, brothers and sisters, until the Lord's coming. See how the farmer waits for the land to yield its valuable crop, patiently waiting for the autumn and spring rains. You too, be patient and stand firm, because the Lord's coming is near."

We tend to believe it's not as simple as to just decide to be patient, but God's Word is telling us it is. Just decide to be patient. Your flesh will hate it at first. It will rebel against patience, but eventually, it will surrender to what He is establishing in you.

The Greek word for patience means to be long-fused or long-tempered. Exercising this kind of patience means setting the timer for your life to God's time, not your time. The James 5 passage above says to be patient "until the Lord's coming." How long do I need to be patient? Until the Lord comes.

Is James talking about the second coming of Christ, or is he talking about the intermediate coming of the Lord when He comes to deliver you out of the trial? I believe this verse represents the latter, His intermediate coming. This is the moment where He invades your situation to deliver you so you can receive the spiritual harvest, the crop that was planted through exercising His patience. This is where you receive His miracles in your difficult circumstances.

For me, deliverance came at the formal end of my obligation. Was the season hard? Yes. Would I do it again for God's glory? Yes. There are countless ways God used that affliction to make me more like Jesus. Patience was cultivated deeper within me in ways I didn't know were possible.

A weak heart doesn't go far in trials. An anemic spiritual life leaves you depleted. You need to be strengthened spiritually to exercise patience and handle those external pressures that come. We must be building up constantly, so when the trial hits, we are strong in the Lord.

God has given us examples in Scripture of many faithful servants who faced trials and exercised patience:

Elijah spoke in the name of the Lord, and Jezebel came after him to take his life. God provided spiritual intervention after spiritual intervention in Elijah's life. He didn't totally remove his trials, but He brought encouragement all along the way. God always came through, right on time.

Noah spent 120 years building an ark that he would live on for 378 days with his family and countless animals. He lived in constant uncertainty about what post-ark life would be like and how long it would take to get there.

Jochebed put her baby, Moses, in a basket and sent him floating down river, hoping he would be rescued. She then displayed great patience as she watched her son be named and raised by another woman.

Hosea walked in obedience and married the prostitute the Lord identified to him. He displayed patience in the waiting as he loved, accepted, and forgave his unfaithful wife, honoring how God forgives.

Joseph believed in God's promises to make him a leader of many and patiently lived in slavery and hardship before receiving exactly what God had promised.

It should not be surprising that Paul often encouraged patience in his writings, as in his ministry he was stoned, flogged, beaten, imprisoned, and shipwrecked three times.

And then there's Job. When Job was going through his many trials, God had His hand on it all and only gave a certain amount of permission to Satan. It is the same with our trials. God has His hand on you and your circumstances. Satan has permission in the world, so not all things happening to you are from God, but do you trust God even when you don't understand? Do you trust Him that He is using your trials to teach you? Do you understand that you're not just supposed to read about Job's experiences, but that you're going to live some of Job's experiences? Those trials bring the same kind of maturity that God brought Job through his trials.

These men and women waited and witnessed while they suffered in trials. They remained faithful to God, letting the nature of God influence them. Yes, they messed up and had hard days, but they brought everything back to God and trusted the lessons would come. God desires you to wait and witness during your trials because He is increasing you. He is making new wine in you. He wants you to receive the harvest through your trials.

The Fruit of Goodness and Faithfulness

There was an estate manager who went out early in the morning to hire workers for his land. They agreed on a wage and went to work.

The manager went back three or four times throughout the day, and each time hired more workers for his land. As Jesus told this story, the manager went back as late as five o'clock to hire even more workers for the day. "When the day's work was over, the owner of the vineyard instructed his foreman, 'Call the workers in and pay them their wages. Start with the last hired and go on to the first.'" Every man, no matter how long they had worked that day, received exactly the same pay. (See Matthew 20:8, MSG.)

Frustration passed among those who were hired early that morning. Finally, someone just said what they all were thinking: "This is not right. You have short-changed us! We did most of the work today. We carried the burden. But you treated them as equals in the labor!"

The owner of the field responded, "Friend, I haven't been unfair. We agreed on the wage, didn't we? So take it and go. I decided to give to the one who came last the same as you. Can't I do what I want with my own money? Can't I decide to be generous?"

In another story, a woman was starting her own business and God had said the opening season would be fall. It was August, yet there was no lease signed. The doors were closing on space after space, and then one day, her husband found what seemed to be the perfect space. It was better than all the rest. They got a copy of the lease and planned to pray about it over the weekend with the hope of signing it on Monday. When Monday came, there were unexpected delays in their morning schedule and then obligations that delayed the signing. That afternoon, an email came through indicating that the lease had been signed by another, and the space was no longer available.

Frustration started to boil up in the couple. They begin to feel like they had been robbed of something that was to be theirs. Rather than remaining in those emotions, they took it back to God in prayer. God reminded them that they had asked Him to make it impossible for them to end up in a space that wasn't appointed by Him. He had done just that! He closed the door and made it impossible for them to get a space that was not His best for them. In recognizing what God was doing, their frustration turned to praise and then back into prayer, asking again that He would make it impossible for them to sign any lease that wasn't His best and to open the doors that needed to be open.

Within a few days, a new listing popped up, and it was right across the street from the previous space. It was less expensive and more perfectly suited for their needs. In short order, the lease was signed.

Consider these stories. What do they have in common?

Each story demonstrates an opportunity for the people involved to encounter God's goodness and faithfulness.

In one, His goodness and faithfulness came in the form of extravagant provision. The laborers were paid a full day's wages for one hour's work. In the other, God's goodness and faithfulness came in the form of protection that brought about His provision for the business owner.

Those aren't just stories about other people's lives. We've all experienced the outrageous and unexpected goodness of God. Even more, we experience these blessings every single day. They are constantly poured out over us.

Goodness and faithfulness are in His essential nature. His words are truth, and in the midst of affliction, Satan wants us to doubt this.

God is good when good things happen, and He is still good in times of affliction. In His goodness and faithfulness, God will use affliction to correct areas of our life. God allows affliction to test the genuineness of your faith. James 1:2–4 says, "Consider it pure joy, my brothers and sisters, whenever you face trials of many kinds, because you know that the testing of your faith produces perseverance. Let perseverance finish its work so that you may be mature and complete, not lacking anything."

Will you honor Him in your current circumstances? If you want more of Him, start in your current circumstances. Are you moving by your own will, or are you seeking and yielding to His? James 1:12 (NIV) says, "Blessed is the one who perseveres under trial because, having stood the test, that person will receive the crown of life that the Lord has promised to those who love Him."

God has a desire for you, and it is aligned with the ministry of heaven. That doesn't necessarily mean He wants you to be a pastor or to go to seminary. Ministry is God's assignment for you. Whatever God has for you, the affliction you experience in life will be used to usher in His promises for you if you press into Him. What you overcome in Christ will become a place for you to speak into the lives of others. There are people who have the same affliction, are believing the same lies, have the same strongholds you once had, and need the power of your testimony of God's goodness and faithfulness to empower and encourage them.

The Lord allows affliction to continue our sanctification process, to conform us to the image of Christ. Nothing is wasted in the kingdom. God will use every circumstance to keep us moving toward being conformed to the image of Christ Jesus. Romans 8:28–29 (NIV) says, "And we know that in all things God works for the good of those who love Him, who have been called according to His purpose. For those God foreknew He also predestined to be conformed to the image of His Son, that he might be the firstborn among many brothers and sisters."

The Fruit of Self-control

Exercising self-control in alignment with the rest of the fruits of the Spirit helps you become more sensitive to the Holy Spirit and to hear Him as He increases your awareness of God's nature in the midst of your circumstances. The Holy Spirit empowers you to settle down and be still so you can exercise self-control and create a space in your heart for His perspective to become your perspective. Self-control is a protective place in the Spirit where you can think, focus, and get aligned with who God wants to be for you rather than with the circumstance you face.

Self-control needs to be cultivated like all fruits of the Spirit. Self-control is not willpower. Willpower is self-focused control from your soul, where your own will is housed. Self-control is in the nature of God, fruit of the Spirit, placed in your spirit. Exercising self-control is the practice of responding to God's nature within rather than letting emotion charge us headfirst into the fights in front of us. Life in Christ is designed to be a demonstration of self-control, where you become fully persuaded that the Holy Spirit is going to teach you who you are in Christ Jesus and give you experiences to exercise what He has given you.

Jesus used self-control all the time, and we can see it when He said in John 5:19 (MSG), "I'm telling you this straight. The Son can't independently do a thing, only what He sees the Father doing. What the Father does, the Son does. The Father loves the Son and includes Him in everything He is doing." Imagine the cost if Jesus went rogue from the Father's plans. Jesus' earthly purpose was to redeem the world, and every conversation, every lesson taught, every word of encouragement, and every use of His authority was a demonstration of the Father's heart, timing, plans, and desires. Jesus changed the world by honoring what the Father asked Him to do. God has a plan for you to change the world too.

> **The price we pay for not exercising self-control is expensive and time consuming. Not exercising self-control leads to the free reign of worldly patterns that persuade you that you are in control but end up exercising control over you.**

Self-control is the discipline of delaying impulse or gratification for a greater purpose or cause. When you exercise self-control, you are saying no for the sake of God's bigger and better yes. You are trading something now for something greater in the future.

Paul uses the metaphor of training for a sporting event as a practical application of self-control that we can still apply to our life today. First Corinthians 9:25–27 (NIV) says, "Everyone who competes in the games goes into strict training. They do it to get a crown that will not last, but we do it to get a crown that will last forever. Therefore I do not run like someone running aimlessly; I do not fight like a boxer beating the air. No, I strike a blow to my body and make it my slave so that after I have preached to others, I myself will not be disqualified for the prize."

Paul is encouraging us to exercise self-control like an athlete, but to maintain our focus on the eternal goal rather than a temporary goal. From a worldly perspective, the messaging of "use your willpower" or "exercise some self-control" usually ends up with people spending their lives fighting temptations and urges by their own strength but never really being free from them. God's way is the complete opposite. What Paul is saying is to remember "the crown that will last forever"—keep your eyes on the true prize—so you can move by the promptings of the Holy Spirit toward God's plan.

When I was first beginning to understand about self-control, the Father was faithful to give me several opportunities to exercise it. Before God pulled us out of our friendships, there was a night when my husband and I went out to dinner with three other couples. I had three beers and realized by the second one that I no longer had boundaries in my thoughts or my words. I was loose-lipped, and I regretted almost everything that came out of my mouth. I was experiencing the conviction of the Holy Spirit about this profoundly, yet I was ignoring it for the sake of a good time out. The next morning, however, my heart was heavy, and I was confident this was something in my relationship with Jesus that needed to be addressed. As I pursued Him in my quiet time, I felt the prompting of the Holy Spirit to do a thirty-day alcohol fast. I came into agreement with this prompt knowing there was something He was wanting to teach me.

Living in the Spirit means turning away from sin and following His lead toward righteousness by praying continually, fasting, worshiping, and remaining in fellowship with other believers. The Holy Spirit shows us what we are missing when we live outside of Him. We can choose to ignore His prompts toward the narrow road—it's definitely not the easy path. The narrow road requires self-evaluation, reconciliation to Christ, and redirection. The narrow road requires us to remove ourselves from our selfish culture. If we do choose to ignore His prompts, we also choose to miss His blessings. Obedience is required for us to receive what God has for us.

About twenty-five days into my thirty-day fast, I went to another event with a group of friends and drank too much. Reflecting on it the next morning, I saw that I had failed to spend time with God that day. I was so preoccupied with all the stuff I had to do that I put Him on the back burner all day, and as a result, I broke my fast and disobeyed what He had asked me to do. God began revealing to me that I was idolizing alcohol and environments where alcohol was prevalent. I had made Him second fiddle to booze. Simultaneously, He was showing me that my body was rejecting the booze, as I always felt like junk after drinking. Yet, I continually chose to drink anyway. I had habits and desires that were conflicting with what my body could tolerate and what Jesus was doing in me. I needed to learn to exercise self-control with booze.

Sometimes you may feel that you fail in the cultivation of the fruit of the Holy Spirit within you. But it is in taking it back to God and receiving the fullness of His lesson for you where you continue to encounter His faithfulness and increase in your understanding of Him. It is also where He can reveal His divine purposes in a given circumstance. Cultivating fruit is a journey that is ongoing. We will mess up, but how we respond when we mess up is what separates those who receive God's fullness from those who do not.

Exercising self-control has tremendous power in your life. Self-control protects your soul by keeping the enemy from gaining a foothold over you. Proverbs 25:28 (NIV) says, "Like a city whose walls are broken through is a person who lacks self-control." The effects of booze on my body, my loose lips, and my distracted mind were taking down my defenses, breaking my city wall, and leaving me vulnerable to the enemy.

Exercising godly self-control helps us pursue a greater eternal good. Paul discusses this in 1 Peter 4:7 (ESV): "The end of all things is at hand; therefore be self-controlled and sober-minded for the sake of your prayers." Ruling over our impulses and actions is one way we remain watchful, sober-minded, and readied for Christ. Exercising self-control allows for God's words and plans to unfold in every circumstance we encounter, establishing His eternal good for us and for those in our sphere of influence. When I drank, I became a vessel for the enemy rather than a vessel for good use. While I wasn't committing major crimes or physically hurting another, I would use negative language and dwell in negative thoughts, inhibiting God's nature from being represented.

Titus 2:11–13 (NIV) says, "For the grace of God has appeared that offers salvation to all people. Grace teaches us to say "No" to ungodliness and worldly passions, and to live self-controlled, upright and godly lives in this present age, while we wait for the blessed hope—the appearing of our great God and Savior, Jesus Christ." God's grace covers you. Remember that promise, because you will mess up, and you will need His grace when you do. Let that grace teach you so you can live more like Him and can be an influence for His kingdom.

How do you cultivate self-control?

- Remain in God's Word.

- Pray for help. Philippians 4:13 (NIV) says, "I can do all this through Him who gives me strength."

- Confess negative habits to God and others for direction and loving accountability.

- Identify and remove the things that tempt you.

- Repent and remember the truth when you fail. Hebrews 4:16 (ESV) says, "Let us then with confidence draw near to the throne of grace, that we may receive mercy and find grace to help in time of need."

You have an accuser, Satan, who hates you and works to condemn and accuse you. Revelation 12:10 (NIV) discusses his access to the throne of God where he accuses you day and night. You have a Savior who gives you what you need to take away Satan's ammunition against you.

Condemnation says, "You're a lost cause" and can cause people to move back into darkness. It is different from conviction, which is the grieving of the Holy Spirit within us as a result of our sin (Ephesians 4:30). Both condemnation and conviction cause us to grieve, but one leads to death and the other leads to life (2 Corinthians 7:8–10). In my circumstance, I felt and responded to the conviction of the Holy Spirit, while also being aware of Satan's attempt to condemn me for messing up.

Condemnation won't point you to Christ and the gospel. Rather, it keeps pointing you back to yourself and your sin. When you're being condemned, you feel strongly that something must change, but you have no helpful ideas about what to do, and you feel burdened rather than encouraged. Condemnation is always a lie for Christians. Conviction is clear and gives you a path out toward repentance and restoration with Jesus. Conviction is the Holy Spirit getting your attention to bring protection, provision, correction, and blessing.

The Fruit of Gentleness

It's dangerous to assume culture or individuals have a valid concept of gentleness. Knowing God's nature and living for Jesus is not about listing a bunch of verses that mention gentleness and being content with that. It's a common error to search online and read the first thing that pops up with a definition of the cultural perspective of a word like gentle, and apply it to God. In our limitless capacity to self-deceive, we can easily take up those cultural perspectives and confuse style and personality with character. Establishing gentleness is not accidental or a style of relating.

I believe that gentleness is the presence of authority under patience and self-control. In Hebrew translations, gentleness commonly means moral goodness, kindness, meekness, excellence in character or demeanor, and humility. These descriptors represent the lens of gentleness God desires us to take up. Instead of seeing gentleness as excellence in character, many misinterpret it as weakness, ineffectiveness, or fragility. God's gentleness is a godly strength that keeps our hearts open to God's nature, even under provocation, in a way that we cannot avoid encountering His peace and unmeasurable love for us. The more time we spend with God, the more our mindsets become soaked in His truth and the more we begin to understand His gentle nature. It's from this posture toward God that we will start to understand gentleness as David did, directly associated with God's protection and provision.

David writes in Psalm 18:35 (NKJV), "You have also given me the shield of Your salvation; Your right hand has held me up, Your gentleness has made me great."

Gentleness and greatness are working in cooperation here. David credits God's gentleness as the source of his greatness. God's protection (the shield) and God's provision (His right hand) are a demonstration of His gentleness to David. God's gentleness is designed to be that for us as well.

Proverbs 15:1 (NIV) says, "A gentle answer turns away wrath, but a harsh word stirs up anger."

In Matthew 11:29 (NIV) Jesus says, "Take my yoke upon you and learn from me, for I am gentle and humble in heart, and you will find rest for your souls."

Jesus is incapable of being frustrated with you. You will never hear frustration and agitation in His voice. You will always hear His gentle nature, with a generous invitation to lay down your burdens and find rest in Him. Gentleness turns away the harshness of anger and positions us into greatness with God, inviting peace, rest, and greatness for God's glory. As we continue to mature in Christ, we can become expectant that all of His interactions with us will come from His gentleness. This knowledge silences the lie of condemnation and judgment that are often wrongly associated with the Lord and affirms that He patiently and gently pursues us as we walk out our sanctification process in Christ.

After Adored Boutique opened, I was in a season of learning to listen and respond to the Holy Spirit in a new way. The more I learned, the more I began to see that I didn't yield to Him enough in my early planning. My lack of yielding to Him was primarily around Adored's budget. Although it's a little easier now, it is humbling to admit that I ignored paying attention to a budget. As a result, I found myself in the quiet of a post-Christmas winter retail season with over $70,000 in inventory sitting in my storage room.

Amid those blustery winter days, I found myself on my knees seeking the Lord in confession, repentance, and understanding about what I got wrong. I longed to know how God saw this circumstance. I began to hear God express a desire to be invited into the decisions I make for the store—including the economic ones. I started to understand that He had protection and provision for me that would manifest if I began engaging Him in those decisions. I wanted His provision, so I changed my purchasing habits. I started praying about what products to order, how many, and from what brands. God overwhelmed my circumstances and every time He spoke, I could hear His gentleness. Regardless of my failure, I knew that I was His daughter, I was adored and totally and completely loved by Him.

After coming back into alignment with the Lord, I began questioning if I had derailed the ministry of His heart for me. In prayer one afternoon, I asked, "Did I miss the opportunity to do this with you?" I held my breath and awaited an answer. In His gentleness, He responded, "No. We can still do it. It's just going to look a little different." I walked away from that encounter full of joy, overwhelmed by His gentleness, and confident in the next steps.

Within a few months, I conducted a business health assessment. My mentor reported, "You need to stop carrying shoes and I want you to seriously consider being open on Sundays." Both comments elicited an emotional response within me. I wasn't prepared for either of these decisions, but I honored my agreement with God and I asked Him what He thought. When I asked Him about being open on Sundays, He responded, "Will you stop worshiping me if you're open on Sundays?" I responded, "Absolutely not." As I reviewed the cost associated with carrying footwear, it was obvious to me that it wasn't a benefit for the business at the time. Although I didn't hear directly from the Lord on that point, I had His peace that I was to move forward as my mentor recommended. Over the next few years, I walked out God's strategy, including selling all the products in my storage room for the price I paid. It was painful not to generate profit, yet encouraging to see the initial investment slowly return. By late 2019, I had liquidated everything in my storage room, no longer had footwear, and enjoyed being open on Sundays. In addition, the Lord gently nudged me to ask two very generous people to help us pay down our start-up debt. As a result of their generosity, when the world shut down in 2020, Adored Boutique was debt-free with no product sitting in storage. To sustain through that season, I again sold everything for the price I paid and as a result, met all my 2020 business expenses, despite being closed for ten weeks.

Like David, we must experience God's gentleness up close and personal at some point. It establishes an expectancy of how He will always talk to us and helps us better understand who He is and who He wants to be for us. Although God was correcting me in that encounter, His gentleness was so prominent that my heart was softened to the correction and I longed to please Him by my obedience. We need to surrender to His perspective over our own, or what other people have given us. If we want to begin living as He desires, we need to hear His gentleness, when He speaks and in His written word. His gentleness ushers in all His other attributes and they partner together to bring forth His nature, through us, into this broken world.

In the process of preparing *When Jesus Shows Up In Skinny Jeans* for publishing, the Lord directed me to invite seven people to read the manuscript. I read it multiple times as well. In the days just before the final steps, I observed that the entire fruit of the Spirit, gentleness, was missing from the text. It was in the chapter title, but there was no content about gentleness. Further, no one caught it! As I sought the Lord about how and why that happened, He spoke to my heart, "What sometimes appears to be a delay is My gentleness on display." I understood what He was saying. Most of the content for this book was developed in 2018 when I began preparing to teach it in my Designed To Be course. At that time, my lens of His gentleness was different than it is today. In 2018, I couldn't see what He was planning to do with the economy of the store, my debt, and all the challenging circumstances that would give me new opportunities to experience His gentleness up close and personal. It was His divine orchestration that the seven didn't catch it so that you could hear the fullness of my testimony. God is this intentional for you, in all of your circumstances. He longs for you to experience His gentleness up close and personal.

Generosity

While generosity is not a fruit of the Spirit, it is an attribute of God that manifests as we cultivate His fruit through our circumstances. The Greek word for generosity is *eumetadotos*. It is a presumed derivative of *metadidomi*: "good at imparting," and is defined as "ready to impart." *Eumetadotos* is further explained as giving from a liberal (generous) attitude that is ready to share, reach out, be spontaneous, give willingly, be open-handed, and joyfully make one's wealth useful to others.

Embracing true generosity can be difficult. Christians tend to live pretty close-fisted and often are suspicious of anyone who encourages us to give away what's "ours." It's not that we doubt that Christians should practice generosity, but our human tendency is to want to measure how generous we need to be. Always wanting someone to spell it out is living under the Law, before Jesus. The thoughts in this mindset sound something like, "How much do I have to give to keep God happy?" It's so much easier to be given an expectation, a plan, a schedule for generosity than to be told to just give as much as you can.

God does not want you to give from a place of obligation, fear, or guilt, but rather, to be so inspired by Jesus' generosity toward you that you want to be equally generous to God's kingdom on earth. In His ministry, Jesus demonstrated and encouraged generosity that the world views as foolish. If you follow Him, He will encourage you to be equally generous, willing, and ready to give as much as you can.

Leviticus 25:35–37 (NIV) says, "If any of your fellow Israelites become poor and are unable to support themselves among you, help them as you would a foreigner and stranger, so they can continue to live among you. Do not take interest or any profit from them, but fear your God, so that they may continue to live among you. You must not lend them money at interest or sell them food at a profit." God was teaching the principles of generosity to the Israelites here. He commanded the Israelites to be generous and merciful to each other, and that it was not acceptable to capitalize another's need for personal gain. God was directing them to show the same kind of generosity to one another that He showed to them in delivering them from captivity.

There is a covenant that exists between God and those who are generous for His glory. Psalm 41:1–3 (NIV) acknowledges this covenant and proclaims that God responds to His sons and daughters moving in His nature with kindness and generosity toward others by bringing His protection and provision. "Blessed are those who have regard for the weak; the Lord delivers them in times of trouble. The Lord protects and preserves them—they are counted among the blessed in the land—He does not give them over to the desire of their foes. The Lord sustains them on their sickbed and restores them from their bed of illness."

In the New Testament, God's messaging about generosity continues to inspire the church to cultivate the true generous and immeasurable nature of God. Luke 6:37–38 (NIV) says, "Do not judge, and you will not be judged. Do not condemn, and you will not be condemned. Forgive, and you will be forgiven. Give, and it will be given to you. A good measure, pressed down, shaken together and running over, will be poured into your lap. For with the measure you use, it will be measured to you."

God is developing a heart of generosity within you that is designed to not only be an extension of generosity, and the fruit of the Spirit within, but also to create in you a level of integrity in all your dealings that represents God's generosity toward you. We see an example of this in the life of King David in 2 Samuel 24. David sinned against the Lord, and as a result, both David and those under his authority were experiencing the consequences of his sin. Those around us will always be affected by our obedience or disobedience. David was instructed to build an altar to the Lord as a demonstration of his submission to God in order to be restored to God and put an end to the consequences of his sin.

David was sent to the threshing floor of Araunah to build the altar. He approached Araunah while he was working at his threshing floor. In reverence to his king, Araunah responded by bowing and asking, "Why has my lord the king come to his servant?" He offered to his king, David, whatever he wanted from the threshing floor. Araunah pointed out everything from his oxen to the ox yokes, saying, "Your Majesty, Araunah gives all this to the king." Araunah also said to him, "May the Lord your God accept you."

David responded to Araunah's generosity with more generosity. Although he could have taken what was being offered at no cost, he refused, and insisted on paying a fair price for what he was going to use. "No, I insist on paying you for it. I will not sacrifice to the Lord my God burnt offerings that cost me nothing." He knew he could not authentically step back into alignment with the Lord without demonstrating the nature of the Lord in the process.

Verses 24–25 (NIV) say, "So David bought the threshing floor and the oxen and paid fifty shekels of silver for them. David built an altar to the Lord there and sacrificed burnt offerings and fellowship offerings. Then the Lord answered his prayer on behalf of the land, and the plague on Israel was stopped." This is how God calls His children to represent His nature and live generously. God does not get upset about you being too generous. There is no measure to His generosity, so in Christ, there should be no measure to yours.

Fruit of the Spirit Summary

God won't force His nature upon you. He allows your free will, but He so longs for you to experience more of Him. His fruit has been fully given to you and is fully available to you right here and right now.

Galatians 6:1 (NIV) says, "Brothers and sisters, if someone is caught in a sin, you who live by the Spirit should restore that person gently. But watch yourselves, or you also may be tempted." When we're moving in the Spirit, we get to partner with the kingdom and help fallen sisters and brothers in Christ become restored to God. It is the demonstration of His true nature that makes way for the conviction of the Holy Spirit, bringing those who are lost into a place of confession, repentance, and deliverance so they can receive God's redeeming grace offered through Christ Jesus. People get turned off when we operate outside of the nature of God.

Isaiah 60:1–3 (NIV) says, "Arise, shine, for your light has come, and the glory of the Lord rises upon you. See, darkness covers the earth and thick darkness is over the peoples, but the Lord rises upon you and His glory appears over you. Nations will come to your light, and kings to the brightness of your dawn." You have a crown in Christ Jesus, and you are loved and valued no matter what. Rise from your difficult circumstances in gratitude for what He has given you and who He calls you to be. Stepping into the fullness of His nature, the fruit of His Spirit, is a decision of the heart, not a result of circumstances.

Prayer: "Father God, I thank you that you have placed the full measure of your nature within me. I did not receive only a portion of you, but I have received all of you because of the blood of Jesus that covers me and the gift of the Holy Spirit. I believe what your Word tells me and that I have the fullness of the fruit of the Holy Spirit within me. Thank you, Father, for this gift. Thank you, Holy Spirit, that you partner with Jesus and empower me into all the things God has for me. I want your fruit to grow in me more. I ask you to forgive me for any sin, willful or unintentional, that has interfered with the cultivation of your fruit in me, and I ask you to reveal those things so I can repent and be forgiven. Help me change my habits so I can grow in your nature. Amen."

CHAPTER 6

Appreciating Anointing and Baptism

I am confident the Father wants to release something more within you. I hope you have that same confidence. Exercising more of your authority in Christ Jesus through the worshipful act of anointing is a powerful part of releasing God's purposes and favor into your life.

While the Father was preparing me for my future in ministry with Him, He taught me about the power of anointing. I had heard this word in my church life, but I had never understood what it was about or seen it done. The more I learned, the more I began wanting to experience His anointing in my life. I was still leading a church Bible study at this time, and as I prayed for the women in it and the church at large, God began weaving into my heart a new perspective.

In our many years in this church body, I had witnessed, but hadn't realized, the tendency for congregants to seek the leading of a human rather than the leading of the Father. Many mourned the leaving of leaders because that person became an idol to them. In this revelation, the Lord also began showing me that His call for us to exit, and for me to delegate this role, was established in His protection and provision for me and the women. He was protecting them from putting any of their hope in me or seeking me as a leader, and providing another opportunity for them to seek God in the midst of change (1 Corinthians 3:21, 1 Corinthians 4:1-4).

The Father affirmed all of this and brought a strategic plan for me in a dream. In summary, I was to briefly teach on anointing, share that God is calling us to worship in a different setting, to prepare this space for future leadership, to anoint the women in the Bible study, and to have them help me anoint the church building. I was a bit nervous about this request. This was a congregation that did not talk about the Holy Spirit, let alone demonstrate His power. It operated like a typical Western church: big God, small Jesus, and no Holy Spirit. I spent a few days preparing with the Lord for this because I needed the plans to be confirmed by Him.

When the day came, He showed up big time. Although I could feel the discomfort in the atmosphere, the women were very willing to experience God in this way and to step out in faith. I proceeded as God directed, and then we each put oil on our hands and walked to every door, the sanctuary, all its elements, and the pastor's office. We spoke an anointing and proclamation over each item and space. The Spirit stirred in several women and brought bold prayers through them. I guarantee this was a first for most of them, and if not a first, it had been a long time since it was done in this building. Many felt a palpable physical shift in the atmosphere as God reclaimed the ground for His kingdom purposes.

I do not fully know what God did in and through the anointing, as a few short weeks later we ended up leaving this congregation, but I did the fullness of what God wanted me to do to prepare that space and those women for what was next. It was and is up to them to continue pressing into God to receive what He has for them, but the stage was set, and God used me to make a way for His Spirit to enter.

Thayer's Greek Lexicon states that anointing is "enduing Christians with the gifts of the Holy Spirit." The act of anointing sets something or someone apart, makes it holy, sacred, and consecrated to God for His purposes. Anointing is designed to empower people to accomplish God's work, and it establishes His authority and protection over something. Anointing also describes the Messiah, Jesus Christ, the Anointed One. Anointing can occur physically by using oil to anoint something or someone. It can also occur spiritually by making proclamations and partnering with the Holy Spirit to anoint something or someone.

In Scripture, anointing was used in both common practice and religious practice. Psalm 23:5 (NIV) says, "You prepare a table before me in the presence of my enemies. You anoint my head with oil; my cup overflows." In common practice, shepherds anointed sheep's heads with oil to prevent sunstroke and parasites. This is what the psalmist is referring to when he says, "you anoint my head with oil." Anointing was also a customary part of the preparation for a feast and a mark of respect sometimes paid by a host to his guests. The psalmist refers to this kind of anointing when he says, "You prepare a table before me." We see a rarer anointing of this kind demonstrated by the sinful woman anointing Jesus' feet in Luke 7:38.

Anointing was a rite of inauguration into the Jewish offices of the prophets, priests, and kings to set them apart. Prophets were occasionally anointed to their office and were sometimes called "anointed" (1 Chronicles 16:22, Psalm 105:15). Priests entering the Levitical priesthood were anointed to their offices (Exodus 40:15, Numbers 3:3).

Anointing was the principal and divinely appointed ceremony in the inauguration of the Jewish kings, sometimes performed more than once. David was anointed three times.

Inanimate objects were also anointed with oil and set apart for religious service. We see anointing in all of the elements of the tabernacle (God's dwelling place) as directed by God in Exodus 30:26–28 (NIV): "Then use it to anoint the tent of meeting, the ark of the covenant law, the table and all its articles, the lampstand and its accessories, the altar of incense, the altar of burnt offering and all its utensils, and the basin with its stand."

Anointing was used for the recovery of the sick. James 5:14 (NIV) says, "Is anyone among you sick? Let them call the elders of the church to pray over them and anoint them with oil in the name of the Lord." The word "sick" is often associated in our minds with a physical illness, but in Scripture, it also refers to spiritual sickness. We see this in Revelation 3:18 (NIV): "I counsel you to buy from me gold refined in the fire, so you can become rich; and white clothes to wear, so you can cover your shameful nakedness; and salve to put on your eyes, so you can see." Jesus is pursuing the Laodiceans and counseling them in what to buy. He closes His counsel by telling them to buy an "eye salve" that will allow them to see spiritually. The Laodiceans understood Jesus was saying they no longer needed to do what they have been doing, go to the occultists to get their eye salve. They only need to go to Jesus. Jesus' salve is the anointing for our spiritual condition.

The power and purposes of anointing has not gone away. Just as in Old Testament and New Testament uses of anointing, it is still a powerful act in our practice as Christians today. Anointing is a tradition that God honors. The act of anointing with oil is much like an electrical appliance that needs to be plugged into a power source in order to work. As a spiritual tool, anointing is powerless without our heavenly Father. God Himself chose the prophets, priests, and kings of ancient Israel according to His favor and to bring about His purposes. He gave instruction for them to be anointed with oil as an act of consecrating them for their office, setting them apart, and activating the power of the Spirit of God. In the new covenant with God, through Christ Jesus, He did the same for all of us. Luke 4:18 tells us that Jesus is anointed Prophet, Priest, and King.

> Daniel 9:25 (NIV): "Jesus, the Messiah yet to come, is referred to as 'the Anointed One'."

> 1 John 2:20 (NIV): "But you have an anointing from the Holy One, and all of you know the truth."

Jesus was anointed by God (Acts 10:38). Therefore, when we receive Jesus, we share in His anointing (2 Corinthians 1:21). This promise positions us to also share in His prophetic, priestly, and kingly offices.

In Christ, we receive a prophetic anointing to hear from God and speak the good news about Jesus, a priestly anointing to pray and worship, and a kingly anointing for the battle against temptation, sin, and evil.

First John 2:27 (NIV) says, "As for you, the anointing you received from Him remains in you, and you do not need anyone to teach you.

But as His anointing teaches you about all things and as that anointing is real, not counterfeit—just as it has taught you, remain in Him."

The anointing we receive from Christ abides in us as we abide in Him, thus setting us in alignment with the will of the Father and Jesus' victory. When we receive the Holy Spirit, we also receive His anointing. The indwelling of the Holy Spirit seals us in the promises of God for life. The Holy Spirit's anointing is different from His indwelling. In Acts 1:8 (NIV), Jesus says, "But you will receive power when the Holy Spirit comes on you; and you will be my witnesses in Jerusalem, and in all Judea and Samaria, and to the ends of the earth."

Indwelling and the anointing of the Holy Spirit are distinct experiences meant for different purposes. The disciples' experience of the indwelling of the Holy Spirit is stated in John 20:22 (NIV): "And with that He breathed on them and said, 'Receive the Holy Spirit.'" At this point, the disciples were born again, and their spirits were alive in Christ Jesus. Jesus then told them that when He departs, they would receive power after the Holy Spirit comes upon them (Acts 1:8), but it was not until the day of Pentecost (Acts 2) that they received the anointing of the Holy Spirit and began to actively function and operate in the power of the Holy Spirit. An anointing of the Holy Spirit is when His power becomes the sanctifying agent that allows us to operate and function in His gifts.

In Christ, with the Holy Spirit, we are all conduits of the power of Christ. But there are some who will receive a fresh anointing of the Holy Spirit and the presence of the Holy Spirit over them, their ministry, or some of their abilities, to accomplish something for God's glory.

A fresh anointing of the Holy Spirit and His empowerment can come through an encounter with God in His Word, through prayer, during worship, and in the act of releasing the negative in exchange for His positive. A fresh anointing can also come through close association with people who carry the integrity, attributes, gifts, and spiritual DNA God has called us to have in our own lives. We see this evidenced in 2 Kings 3:11 (NIV), where three kings are seeking the wisdom of the Lord: "But Jehoshaphat asked, 'Is there no prophet of the Lord here, through whom we may inquire of the Lord?' An officer of the king of Israel answered, 'Elisha son of Shaphat is here. He used to pour water on the hands of Elijah.' Jehoshaphat said, 'The word of the Lord is with him.'" Elisha was serving Elijah, and in saying "he poured water on his hands," Jehoshaphat was acknowledging that Elisha served Elijah and that the mantle (prophetic authority) that was on Elijah now rests on Elisha. Some biblical scholars interpret Elijah's placing of his cloak on Elisha as an act of anointing him as his successor as prophet to Israel. In 1 Kings 19:16 (NIV), God says to Elijah, "Also, anoint Jehu son of Nimshi king over Israel, and anoint Elisha son of Shaphat from Abel Meholah to succeed you as prophet." After Elijah dies, Elisha anoints Jehu with oil.

This is what we read on Elisha's anointing. 1 Kings 19:19-20 (NIV) "So Elijah went from there and found Elisha son of Shaphat. He was plowing with twelve yoke of oxen, and he himself was driving the twelfth pair. Elijah went up to him and threw his cloak around him. Elisha then left his oxen and ran after Elijah. 'Let me kiss my father and mother goodbye,' he said, 'and then I will come with you.'"

In 2 Kings 1, when Elijah is taken to heaven, his cloak (mantle) falls to the ground and Elisha uses it to part the Jordan River. Elisha was pursuing God and anointed for his role before the mantle of Elijah was given to him. This is similar to David. He was anointed as a teenager as God's chosen king for Israel. He didn't take the throne, however, until more than a decade later.

Sometimes we anoint in faith or anoint based on God's promise, but the fulfillment of that anointing isn't clear for days, years or even decades.

Elisha's story is where we get the phrase, "the passing of the mantle." The mantle that is on the person or the house you serve may be placed upon you. It's not automatic just because you hang out with the person. It's all about intimacy, pursuing God, and being active in relationship with Him.

In the New Testament, we see the other side of this play out with Judas. Judas was part of the call of God, he was present with Jesus and the disciples, but he had a heart of betrayal. Jesus knew Judas' heart, yet He allowed him to remain in the ministry as they cast out demons and walked with Him. Judas moved in the empowerment of the Holy Spirit and was involved in the casting out of demons, but he did not have salvation. If you have empowerment but no salvation, what good is it? If you have salvation, but no empowerment of the Holy Spirit, you are minimizing and missing all the opportunities God has for you on this side of heaven. Ultimately, it's about relationship, and if you choose to not pursue intimacy with Jesus, you're simultaneously choosing to not receive this massive provision, the gift Jesus has for you.

Judas chose to not move in intimacy. He chose betrayal and rebellion against God. He missed Jesus in skinny jeans. God protected those Judas ministered to, and He did not withhold His blessing from them because of Judas' sin, but Judas missed it. One without the other, empowerment without salvation or salvation without empowerment, is not of God. There's a distortion of this truth that Satan has been spreading through the church for generations. Like with love and truth, you cannot lead with love and not have truth and call it love. You also cannot lead in truth and not have love and say it's truth.

Jesus encourages us in Matthew 7:23 (NIV) that it is all about the intimacy of the relationship. Those who are false, who are showing up and looking the part outwardly but do not know Jesus, will not fool Jesus. "Then I will tell them plainly, 'I never knew you. Away from me, you evildoers!'"

I mentioned the common practice of pouring oil on sheep. The bugs that irritate sheep will travel up the sheep's nose and lay eggs, which turn into worms that can burrow into the animal's brain. The sheep will bang their heads on trees, rocks, posts, or brush, trying to get rid of the irritation, and they can die from this. The oil the shepherd pours each day on the sheep's nose acts like a lubricant to cause the bugs to slide out instead of flying in.

As Christians, steering along the trials of our earthly journeys, we need the oil of the Holy Spirit daily. While pursuing the ministry of the Father's will for us, we need a regular fresh outpouring, a fresh anointing, to calm the challenges, to shed light on our circumstances, to protect us from the onslaught of the enemy, and to bring divine healing. The Holy

Spirit acts like a salve for us, keeping us from being taken down by trials and repelling negative and demonic influences that try to attack us.

There are some requirements with anointing. We can't just go around anointing things and claiming that it has more value than it does. We cannot anoint ourselves and then claim to be all-powerful. God delegates authority, and His authority is given to us through Christ Jesus at salvation. Godly authority is not based on anointing. It's important to understand the Scriptures' use of "anoint" in order to understand how anointing works in the new covenant with Christ.

We can anoint ourselves as demonstrated in Scripture with grooming and skincare practices. Ruth 3:3 (NASB) says, "Wash yourself therefore, and anoint yourself, and put on your best clothes, and go down to the threshing floor…." The meaning of "anoint" here is like saying, "Put on your makeup to make yourself presentable." Similarly, in Matthew 6:17–18 (ESV), Jesus talks about doing things out of sincere caring instead of to be seen and praised by others: "But when you fast, anoint your head and wash your face, that your fasting will not be seen by others but by your Father.… "

Godly anointing is an act of the Lord. If we anoint material things with oil, it is part of the consecration, the setting-apart, of the object for God's use. By anointing something, we are claiming it for His purposes. Anything outside of the Word of God, His nature, or His purposes is not of God and should therefore not be anointed as such.

When we took over the space God set aside for Adored, the ministry with a storefront God appointed me to, we scheduled an anointing night. We invited about twenty people to come and be part of this tradition with us. We prayed, spoke a brief word about anointing, gave everyone oil, and invited them to touch any surface and proclaim whatever the Lord wanted them to. We had people outside, in the basement, in the bathroom, everywhere, claiming that place as holy unto the Lord. It happened to be a Friday night, and the bar nearby had some heavy traffic, so when someone was standing outside my front door commanding enemy spirits to leave in the name of Jesus, and we all felt one leave the space, it grabbed the attention of a few unsuspecting people.

The ground of this store had just been claimed for the kingdom of God, and everything that had been given permission to be there before we arrived was no longer allowed to be there. After the anointing, we blew a shofar (ram's horn). A shofar was used in Old Testament ceremonies for multiple reasons. For our purposes, it was to signify the Lord going before us in the battle we knew we were entering. I'm not sure if you've ever blown a ram's horn, but it's not easy. My husband had to try a few times to get sound out, but when it came, it was awesome.

All this talk about anointing may have triggered a question in you about the difference between baptism and anointing. The power of a single question can change the trajectory of our life. Our answers to questions are either yes or no. No matter what it is, how we respond to a question will change the trajectory of our life. If you're asking this question about the difference between baptism and anointing, you need to know that God is not afraid of your questions, so press in. The fact that you're asking it may mean that it is time for your life trajectory to change.

Baptism is different from anointing. Baptism is a visual, symbolic demonstration of a person's union with Christ and His death and resurrection. Baptism comes from the Greek word baptizo, which means to cleanse by dipping, submerging, or immersing. Baptism signifies that a person's former way of life has been put to death (under the water) and points to their new life, saved and redeemed by Jesus through His resurrection (coming out of the water).

Baptism does not save you. That can only happen through the grace of Jesus Christ and your faithful acceptance of His sacrifice on the cross for you. Baptism is a powerful symbolic demonstration of a person's acceptance of Christ as their Lord and Savior and their commitment to becoming a disciple of Christ. It models Christ's example, as He chose to be baptized (Matthew 3:13–17). When we do the same, we identify with and obey Jesus. Matthew 28:18–20 (NIV) says, "Then Jesus came to them and said, 'All authority in heaven and on earth has been given to me. Therefore go and make disciples of all nations, baptizing them in the name of the Father and of the Son and of the Holy Spirit, and teaching them to obey everything I have commanded you. And surely I am with you always, to the very end of the age.'"

Some of us were baptized as infants as part of a religious tradition. We can stop there, live a life loving God, be saved by the blood of Jesus, and hold onto that future promise. But ask yourself a question: When someone else makes a choice for me, am I more or less invested in it?

Scripture does not discuss infant baptism, anywhere. It is a religious tradition that humans established. It is not a kingdom of God tradition. I participated in it, both as an infant and for my infant children. As parents, it was a meaningful moment for us, but as we have matured in our faith and in intimacy with Christ Jesus, we have also matured in our understanding about what God's Word says about baptism. If I had another child, I'd do it differently.

In the above Scripture, God is saying that part of His heavenly strategy for you is to help you turn further away from this sick and stupid culture, to decide for Him, and to choose to be baptized. His strategy is designed to increase you in Christ Jesus and the Holy Spirit so you can move into deeper alignment with His heart for you. It is through obedience to these things that you will receive and experience the fullness of life in Christ. Making your own choice to be baptized is an outward symbol, to the world, of the inward transformation that Jesus has done in you.

While on my last Cuba trip, early on I learned there was going to be a Caribbean Sea baptism. Immediately, I heard the Lord say, "I want you to get baptized." In response, I tried to convince God that He was wrong. All week, He pursued me about it, and when the day came, He did not relent. As I packed up my things before we headed out for the day, I heard Him prompt again, "I want you to get baptized today." In rebellion, I ignored Him and intentionally didn't pack a change of clothes so I'd have a reason not to get in the water. Later that day, when we arrived at the beach, as I got out of the van, I felt the Holy Spirit encourage me again to get baptized. Again, I did not engage the message. As we stood on the beach watching things get started, I felt a profound prompting from the Lord to get in line. I responded with my planned exit strategy: "I didn't bring a change of clothes. I cannot possibly go." He didn't care about that. He kept pursuing.

I said, "Lord, I have my purse and phone and nowhere to put it. I cannot go." To which He replied, "I am not letting you miss this blessing." With that, I felt a release of hesitation and fear, a deep and profound joy, and suddenly I had an inexplicable desire to experience what I was watching others do. I wanted to be baptized, and I wanted whatever God wanted to bless me with through the process. Before I knew it, I had handed my bag to another person on the trip, and I was getting into the water.

A group of Cuban pastors had lined up in the water forming an aisle, and the bishop of the church stood at the end. As I walked through the water, each pastor put their hands on my head and prayed over me. I had no idea what they were saying, but I could feel the power of the Holy Spirit surging in my body. I reached the end of the line, where the bishop submerged me in the water and brought me back up.

Something had shifted in me under that water, but I had no idea what it was. What I felt was that more needed to happen—God wasn't done yet. I was wrestling with something in my spirit, but I didn't understand what it was. I couldn't open my eyes, because between the salt water and the reflection of the sun, it was painful, so I just kept them closed as I processed what I was wrestling with. Out of the group of women on the trip with me, I heard the voice of one, Kim, who had been encouraging me all week. She said, "Emily, just receive it." In that moment, I realized I was clenching my fists, stiff-necked, and fighting about what God was trying to free me from. I was wrestling with pride. In response to Kim's words and the Holy Spirit affirming to me that I needed to receive, I released my grip, raised my arms, and shouted, "I receive it" as loud as I could. The physical shift I felt when I popped out of the water went deeper, and not only did I feel a release in my body, I also felt movement in my spirit that I had never felt before. I knew I had just been baptized by the Holy Spirit. Now I needed to figure out what that meant.

In Acts 2:38 (NIV), Peter says, "Repent and be baptized, every one of you, in the name of Jesus Christ for the forgiveness of your sins. And you will receive the gift of the Holy Spirit." Peter is showing us that the way to remove ourselves from our sick culture is to turn to God, be baptized, and receive the Holy Spirit. In other words, move by faith, get dipped into the waters, make a living sacrifice out of your flesh, and be raised out a new person alive in the Spirit of God.

Peter is telling them to make the choice for baptism and to live from the place of the Holy Spirit within. In Acts 2, this call prompted 3,000 people to confess, turn away from rebellion, and claim Jesus for their hope and future, as well as to anchor them deeper to what God had designed faith to be. My decision for baptism was an act of faith that anchored me deeper into who God designed me to be. This outward act of obedience was also a personal commitment I was making to Jesus. It became what I now see as a profound turning point in the intimacy of my relationship with Jesus and in my stepping into the higher calling that He had for me. It was just a few days later that He affirmed He had a kingdom ministry for me if I wanted it.

If you were baptized as an infant or in a time where the decision to be baptized was made for you by your parents or someone else, or you were baptized before you trusted Jesus as your Savior, I encourage you to make that decision for yourself and get baptized at this time. It should be the personal decision of you as an individual to be baptized when you are prompted by the Lord and ready, without pressure from family members or friends. Your motivation should be to please God, not other people. As demonstrated in my testimony, our motivations can transform in the blink of an eye. So while you may not feel motivated now, as you continue pursuing the Holy Spirit, you may find that changes.

Prayer: "Father God, I thank you for the provision you offer us in anointing and baptism. What a blessing it is that we can be set apart for you and your kingdom's purposes. Help me to make sense of this teaching, to understand your heart for me, and to move where you say to move. I trust you, I desire more of you, I want nothing to stand between us. If you desire me to take steps toward anointing or baptism, or both, I invite you to show me, to open the doors and help me to hear you clearly. I do not want to miss the blessing. In Jesus' name I pray. Amen."

CHAPTER 7

Growing in Confession, Repentance, and Responsive Obedience

Despite all my childhood church exposure, I do not remember learning about confession, repentance, and obedience beyond the general understanding. Somehow, I had completely missed that I need to address sin in my life, including the little Christian sins like envy, greed, pride, jealousy, and selfishness. In my current ministry, I find most women with whom I get the privilege of walking also don't know much about confession, repentance, and obedience as a lifestyle with Christ Jesus. In my experience, it's not something that is taught much to new believers. As a result, many Christians live a lifetime separated from God by their unconfessed sin. The truth of life in Christ is that confession, repentance, and obedience are essential commitments we need to learn about and commit to if we want to experience intimate life with Jesus. In pure Jesus style, as I began to become aware of my need for confession and repentance, He met me in skinny jeans and lovingly walked me through the learning.

Deuteronomy 28:1–2 (NIV) contains a prophetic promise of God—a promise for you, that when you remain obedient to His will, you will see these things in your life that are part of His divine response to your obedience. "If you fully obey the Lord your God and carefully follow all His commands I give you today, the Lord your God will set you high above all the nations on earth. All these blessings will come on you and accompany you if you obey the Lord your God." Believing in and desiring God's promise of His favor is a powerful motivation to remain obedient to Him, and who doesn't want all those blessings from God?

Is it possible the reason you are not in a more organic and intimate relationship with God is because of the bad things that have happened in your life or your family's spiritual roots? You may not want to ask this question because it may lead you to an uncomfortable conclusion. But, if you are sincere about your desire to live in the fullness that Jesus offers you—physically, mentally, and spiritually—this is an important question to ask. Spiritually rooted disease tries to rob you of God's prophetic promises. If allowed to take root, at the very least, spiritually rooted disease will interfere with you receiving the full manifestation of God's promises for you. Spiritually rooted disease stems from separation from God at some or all of these three levels:

- From God: His word, His person, and His love

- From self: not accepting self, not loving self, guilt, condemnation

- From others: breached relationships, hatred, bitterness, envy, jealousy, competition, performance, divisiveness, lack of love

The longer a spiritually rooted disease goes on, the harder it becomes to recognize it for what it is and to respond to it in an effective and God-honoring way.

In James 1:13–16 (NIV), the Lord explains the steps we all encounter as we are tempted toward sin. These are the places where Satan is at work to cause us to sin and separate us from God through our disobedience. "When tempted, no one should say, 'God is tempting me.' For God cannot be tempted by evil, nor does He tempt anyone; but each person is tempted when they are dragged away by their own evil desire and enticed. Then, after desire has conceived, it gives birth to sin; and sin, when it is full-grown, gives birth to death."

- "Tempted": Temptation is not yet sin but is always used to introduce sin. Temptation starts as a thought around your weakest link.

- "Dragged away": Being drawn away is a preoccupation with that wrong thought, letting your mind be drawn into it. This is still not sin but moves you closer to it.

- "Own evil desire": Personal lust is the forming of sin. Personal lust/desire is still not physical sin, but it is the start of taking pleasure in the imagination of the sin. You start to weaken and fall into agreement with the sin, thereby justifying it. Ephesians 5:3 (MSG) says, "Don't allow love to turn into lust, setting off a downhill slide into sexual promiscuity, filthy practices, or bullying greed."

- "Enticed": Enticement is when your will weakens, and Satan pursues you to act it out. Your protection comes in James 4:7 (NIV): "Submit yourselves, then, to God. Resist the devil, and he will flee from you."

- "Desire (lust) has conceived": Conceived desire is the birthing of something not yet in place. A weakening will and greater agreement with the temptation is happening. Entrance into the physical of what began as spiritual occurs in this phase, as your total will has yielded to the sin temptation.

- "Birth to sin": Actual sin is when you are one with the sin and fully in agreement with it.

- "Birth to death": Death is the consequence of sin. James 1:15 (NIV) says, "Then, after desire has conceived, it gives birth to sin; and sin, when it is full-grown, gives birth to death."

There are consequences to sin. Just as God is faithful to teach us about the blessings and promises He pours out in response to our fidelity to Him, He is faithful to teach the consequences of sin that come as a result of rebelling against Him. You cannot acknowledge only God's faithfulness, goodness, kindness, love, and mercy without also recognizing His holiness. He cannot be where sin is. Therefore, if you sin without confession and repentance, you are outside of the covering of God and vulnerable to the influences of the enemy.

Deuteronomy 28:15–68 describes "Curses for Disobedience." In these verses, God is teaching the consequences of sin. These are not consequences the Lord will bring upon us, as in the blessings of the first thirteen verses. Rather, the "curses" or consequences of sin are what Satan brings when we have fidelity to him. He is evil, he brings evil. We can't dip our toes in unholiness and expect we won't be affected by it.

Ephesians 6:12 (NIV) says, "For our struggle is not against flesh and blood, but against the rulers, against the authorities, against the powers of this dark world and against the spiritual forces of evil in the heavenly realms."

Second Corinthians 10:3–5 (NIV) says, "For though we live in the world, we do not wage war as the world does. The weapons we fight with are not the weapons of the world. On the contrary, they have divine power to demolish strongholds. We demolish arguments and every pretension that sets itself up against the knowledge of God, and we take captive every thought to make it obedient to Christ."

Open doors to curses, demonic assignments, and cords of sin are some of the consequences of sin. Sin will continue to rule as long as those open doors remain. In order to resolve them permanently and cancel the access Satan has to us, or our circumstances, sin must be confessed, we must repent, and the strongholds must be broken in the authority of Christ Jesus. Until strongholds are broken in God's prescribed way, they are allowed to continue to influence for the purpose of the demonic.

We can fast, pray, and cry out to God for His grace and mercy, and often we do those things. But if a spiritual stronghold was formed in the spirit realm through sin, intentional or unintentional, then the full authority of the blood of Jesus must be exercised so Jesus can deliver you, or another, out of that stronghold.

There is a thrill attached to obedience, and God desires you to find and dwell in it.

The revelation of the Holy Spirit will teach you to recognize the plans Satan has for you and the ways he tries to trick you. As you mature in faith, you'll also begin to see how Satan is scheming against others, your community, your nation, or the world. With maturation in Christ, you'll feel more confident about how to respond accordingly to those revelations of the Holy Spirit. As you abide in Christ, you can frustrate the plans of the enemy and cancel them by Jesus' authority.

As a nation, we have been somewhat robbed of the thrill of taking ground for the kingdom of God. We have become accustomed to hearing messages, doing nothing, not having accountability to change, remaining in mediocrity, and eventually disobeying—so much so that it has become a novelty when someone actually obeys and encounters God in powerful ways. That's not how it is supposed to be. Jesus rose from the dead and said all authority, every ounce of authority, was given to Him, and He then commanded us to go and make disciples.

When your boss gives you an assignment and you choose not to do it, it is a big deal. When we disrespect our Lord, ignore what He is asking us to do, even when we understand the assignment, because we just don't feel like doing it, it's a big deal.

The Son of God is telling us go make disciples, but we have lived our lives never even seriously thinking about doing it. The Lord is calling you to the place where you can encounter the thrill of obedience as you make disciples in the places He assigns you to.

In Acts 20:22–27 (NIV), Paul says, "And now, compelled by the Spirit, I am going to Jerusalem, not knowing what will happen to me there. I only know that in every city the Holy Spirit warns me that prison and hardships are facing me. However, I consider my life worth nothing to me; my only aim is to finish the race and complete the task the Lord Jesus has given me—the task of testifying to the good news of God's grace. Now I know that none of you among whom I have gone about preaching the kingdom will ever see me again. Therefore, I declare to you today that I am innocent of the blood of any of you. For I have not hesitated to proclaim to you the whole will of God." Paul had peace, but He didn't shrink back or withdraw from the hard conversation.

But Paul didn't control it. He knew his role was not to control the response of the audience, just as God does not control us. That is a hard reality when moving in obedience to God. Mark 16:20 tells us that after Jesus ascended, He worked with the disciples. In the same way, He will work with us, and empower us to be witnesses. He understands a disapproving audience's response. It may be rough, our hearts may break, but the presence of Christ will be with us, and nothing compares to that.

Early in our faith relationship with God, often what we need from God is for Him to open our hearts and eyes to what He is doing in the spiritual realm. As we mature in Him, God starts moving in the spiritual realm and prompts us to respond in both the physical and spiritual realms.

Our maturation in Christ, and exercising responsive obedience, develops this intimacy. You'll still feel the temptations that come to your flesh, and in your humanness you will still sin, but your foundation is on the Rock, and your desire for more of God motivates you to stop letting Satan entice you into sin like he used to be able to do.

In the book of Nehemiah, we meet Nehemiah at this place of maturation where he is listening for God prompts through the Spirit, and as God responds, Nehemiah is responsively obedient in both the spiritual and the physical realms. Nehemiah's character was not dictated by his circumstances. Rather, it resulted from intimacy with God and remaining in responsive obedience despite what was coming up against him. Because of this, Nehemiah's faith grew, and God was able to use him.

At the very end of chapter 1, Scripture tells us that Nehemiah's job was cupbearer of the king—a role that only a person regarded as thoroughly trustworthy could hold. This sets the stage for us to understand the nature of the relationship and the heart of service that Nehemiah had for the king. In his responsibility as a servant, Nehemiah was being prepared and positioned by God for even greater work. After learning that Jerusalem, his home, was in ruins, the evidence of Nehemiah's sadness was on his face. In chapter 2, the king learned what was wrong and why Nehemiah was sad, and he asked him, "What is it you want?"

Scripture tells us in Nehemiah 2:4 (NIV) that Nehemiah paused that conversation and "Then I prayed to the God of heaven...." Nehemiah went right back to God, pursuing Him for what He thought about the situation, before answering the king. As a result, He was confident that His answer was in line with the will of the Father. "If it pleases the king and if your servant has found favor in his sight, let him send me to the city in Judah where my ancestors are buried so that I can rebuild it."

The king could have shut it down right here and told Nehemiah, "No way, who is going to do your job here?" But rather, he responded with favor and answered Nehemiah with, "How long will your task take and when would you expect to return?" In his affirmed confidence, Nehemiah went on to request letters for the governors to authorize his travel and the keeper of the king's forest to supply him with timber. The king agreed and gave him all he needed, provision above and beyond, to travel safely and complete his objectives. This was the assignment God had been preparing Nehemiah for, and his blessing was multiplied because of his faithful pursuit of God.

We experience the depth of God's favor when we move in obedience. We know that God's favor does not mean we won't experience trouble.

God never promises us there won't be hardship. In fact, the fruit of His Spirit that He is developing in us speaks to God's wisdom that we will need those attributes. And we see that in Nehemiah's testimony too. Once the process was in play, the enemy forces heard about what God was doing. Nehemiah needed that fruit of the Spirit of God to keep pressing forward into the rest of God's assignment for him.

Surrounding the Jews were the Amorites and Horonites. Generations before, God had driven these groups from the promised land, and they remained enemies of the Jews, seeking for Jerusalem to remain in ruins. When they heard about this promotion of the welfare of the Israelites, they were disturbed and saw it as rebellion against their king, the King of Persia.

The enemy has limited resources. He releases those resources in his frustration whenever he learns that something is happening to bless God's children or manifest God's purposes. Satan thought he had won over Jerusalem in his previous destruction of it, but God had other plans. As we continue to read Nehemiah's story, we see more of the attempts of the enemy to interrupt what God is doing.

In Nehemiah's account of his arriving in Jerusalem, after staying there three days, he set out during the night with a few others. He told no one what God had put in his heart to do for Jerusalem. In obedience, He kept it all between him and God until God released him, in His perfect timing, to speak.

Nehemiah went out alone and scouted the wall at night, and upon returning, God released him to begin sharing with the Israelites. In obedience, he said to them, "You see the trouble we are in: Jerusalem lies in ruins, and its gates have been burned with fire." Then he invites them, "Come, let us rebuild the wall of Jerusalem, and we will no longer be in disgrace." He went on to tell them about the gracious hand of God on him and what the king had done to help him be successful. He was confident it was of God because he had taken it to God, asking and listening. It wasn't just some arbitrary sense that God had this for him. It was confidence because of his intimate relationship with God.

This was all the Jews needed to hear to move into alignment with God's plan. It was God's perfect timing and perfect way. As a result of Nehemiah's obedience, their hearts had been made ready, and they immediately responded in affirmation to start rebuilding.

And the enemy? He responded by mocking Nehemiah and making suggestions that he was rebelling against the king. Nehemiah's obedience to God developed such confidence in God, His ways, and His timing that Nehemiah could face the enemy directly with the same confidence and authority and shut down his attempt to interfere with what God said He wanted to do.

Everyone from the surrounding tribes—the priests and residents of surrounding communities—all labored together to complete the rebuilding. They had gotten to a place in the rebuild where the wall had reached half its original height all the way around. Scripture says the people put their all into it, fully committed to the work because God had appointed it. Nehemiah's obedience made a way for everything else God wanted to do to come into alignment.

Sanballat was the Samaritan leader. He heard about the rebuilding of the wall and became angry and greatly incensed. He began to scheme, mock, and terrorize Nehemiah and the Jews. As a representative of Satan, Sanballat and other leaders who joined him in their frustration over the rebuilding tried to create trouble.

Because Nehemiah and the Israelites were moving in such alignment with God through their obedience to Him, God prompted them in their hearts by the Spirit of God about what the enemy was going to try to do. He went ahead of the plans of the enemy and told His faithful children about them so they could move for the kingdom and frustrate the demonic plans. God also revealed a heavenly strategy for how they were to respond. Nehemiah 2:9 tells us, "But we prayed to our God and posted a guard day and night to meet this threat." God revealed it before it happened, and that allowed for a natural and spiritual reinforcement of God's authority around the perimeter of Jerusalem to deal with the enemy.

The enemy worked overtime to try to sink morale and strike fear and doubt in the Israelites. The tactics he used were physical fatigue, roadblocks exacerbating that fatigue, fear and intimidation about the strength and skill of the enemy, and he even used the Jews from the surrounding areas to reinforce fear and bring doubt, suggesting there was nowhere to hide from the enemy. Today, Satan uses these same tired tactics to try to get us to stop doing what we are doing for God. If he can, he will even try to use other Christians to speak to us out of a place of fear in an effort to derail us.

But God provides in the face of the enemy. When we are moving in responsive obedience, we can stay confident, and we will have the mind of Christ about our circumstances. Nehemiah stationed guards on the wall and spoke encouragement into the leaders to put their minds on God so they could fight for their families and for God's purposes in Jerusalem. In Nehemiah's obedient response, God frustrated the plan of the enemy, and the people of Jerusalem went back to work on the wall for God's glory. Their confidence in God and commitment was restored, and as a result of seeing God's glory on display, they began to align with their new foundation rooted in the testimony of God's faithfulness they had witnessed. They began working with a weapon in one hand and a tool in the other. This encounter with the enemy had brought them to a place of maturity that impacted their approach in the battle. From that day on, half of the men did the work while the other half were equipped with spears, shields, bows, and armor. The officers posted themselves behind all the people who were building the wall. Those who carried materials did their work with one hand and held a weapon in the other, and each of the builders wore his sword at his side as he worked.

Nehemiah had a trumpet blower who remained with him. Nehemiah told the Jews working on the wall that they needed to spread out because of the extensive amount of work to be done. They were widely separated from each other along the wall, so he asked them, when they heard the sound of the trumpet, to come to him. He reinforced that the trumpet will be a sign that God is fighting for them. They were ready for battle. They slept in their clothes with their weapons in hand, keeping watch through the night. This is a demonstration of what readiness in both the physical and spiritual realms looks like!

For us, readiness in Christ Jesus is moving in responsive obedience with God's armor firmly fixed upon us, heavenly weapons in hand (praise, the sword of the Spirit, or another weapon God may give you), and the tools God has given us (the blood of Jesus, authority in Christ, God's Word, spiritual gifts, anointings, the mantles of God) in the other hand. Readiness is overwhelming confidence in Christ even when we don't know if or how the enemy is approaching us. We still stand in readiness, trusting what God has given us.

In Nehemiah's testimony, Satan kept trying. Today, he still keeps trying. When he has ground at risk of being lost, he will try to keep it and to gain new ground.

In the midst of all God was doing, a great protest mounted in the people of Judah about their poverty and previous struggles. The unity and togetherness that was being developed was disrupted by the enemy. All their past problems came out, and they began to complain about how they had to mortgage their vineyards and homes, borrow money to pay taxes, and some even had to sell their children. They were left with a huge debt they will never be able to pay, and with no recourse because someone else owned their property.

Side note: This still happens today. This is how the enemy tricks people into slavery and exploitation and keeps them there. He robs them of all their things, including their spiritual and physical identities, and even selling their children. Every day, people are left with no resources to correct what has been taken from them and find themselves in bondage to the enemy.

Satan took what was true, what the leaders had actually done in the past, and he tried to create strife about it. Satan wanted this discourse to derail what God was doing. But God saw all of this coming. He knew the enemy would make more than one attempt, and he also knew there was more than one thing the enemy had rights to in this body of people that needed to be broken. God took the enemies' attempt to create strife, and instead, He brought truth forward, canceled Satan's permissions, and redeemed the situation.

Nehemiah became indignant and called the nobles and officials on the carpet. He brought God's truth into the situation and held them lovingly accountable. He told them to stop gouging their own people and to give back their foreclosed fields. And they agreed. The spirit of God was upon the circumstance because of Nehemiah's obedience. The enemy's plans to break up what God was doing were intercepted by the truth of God, and His holy desires played out rather than the negative. Satan planned to use it as a downfall, but Nehemiah's willingness to be boldly obedient to God and to provide loving accountability allowed for truth to be spoken and for the redemption of what was broken. What might have been true was redeemed in truth, and Satan felt increasingly threatened by that. When word came to Sanballat, and other leaders joining him in terrorizing the people, that the wall was almost complete, they sent Nehemiah a message inviting him to meet together in one of the villages.

Discerning that they were scheming, he declined. They continued to request to meet, a total of four times. But Nehemiah declined four times. Satan kept trying, but God did not fatigue. A fifth letter was sent by Sanballat, unsealed to strike fear in anyone who might read it. The letter told Nehemiah of a circulating rumor that they were rebuilding the wall because the Jews were planning to rebel and that

Nehemiah wanted to be king, having already appointed prophets to announce him as king of Judah.

Nehemiah made it clear that this was all made up. He could see right through what Satan was doing and honored God with his response, knowing that he was frustrating Satan's plans through his obedience. In response, Satan reorganized his attempts to intimidate Nehemiah and the Israelites into quitting. And again, Nehemiah went back to God and prayed for strength. In the very beginning and in the midst of the battle, it was Nehemiah's pattern to go back to God before responding.

One day, a man came and warned Nehemiah that the enemy was coming to kill him. He told Nehemiah to go hide in the temple. Because of his intimacy with the Father, Nehemiah discerned that this man was not sent by God, that he was working for the enemy and had been hired to intimidate. He did not fall into the trap. Rather, in responsive obedience, Nehemiah went back to God and prayed against the plans of the enemy.

God prevailed, and the wall was completed in fifty-two days. Despite all the attacks and attempts to derail, God completed this in fifty-two days. When the enemy saw it was done, he lost nerve because he knew God was behind it. All attempts to stop, intimidate, and strike fear into people were frustrated because of Nehemiah's steadfast faith and obedience.

God's children who had been exiled and scattered returned to Jerusalem to live and worship there again. Worship of the Almighty was restored among them. They began to praise and honor Him. They began to repent on behalf of their ancestors, who had denied God with their disobedience and rebellious behavior. They broke the curses and strongholds that were attached to them because of generational sin. All of the consequences of behaviors that had occurred in rebellion against God were resolved so they were no longer a barrier between them and God. They acknowledged God's sovereignty, and they acknowledged the consequences of their sin as they proclaimed themselves as bond slaves to the Lord, in His service because their hearts desired to serve Him. They acknowledged all their great distress before God, and through this, everything shifted.

They made a binding agreement, a covenant, with God. They promised to honor His law, to assume responsibility for what God had asked them to do, and to not neglect the house of God. They dedicated the rebuilt wall to the Lord. God revealed curses that had been spoken over His people, hidden things of the enemy that needed to be broken off for them to have the fullness of intimacy with God that He desired for them. God broke those curses and brought a deeper spiritual freedom for the Jews.

It is only through faithful obedience to what God calls us to do, with Him and on His behalf, that we can experience this depth of His favor in our lives. The stakes were high for Nehemiah's call, but because of his servant's heart and faithful obedience, God trusted Him with not only canceling the plans of the enemy and rebuilding Jerusalem, but through that process, also re-establishing a heart for God among its people. God's purpose was so much more than just rebuilding a wall.

God has this degree of important opportunities for you. Life-changing, world-changing, ground-taking-for-the-kingdom-of-God kind of opportunities.

Nehemiah didn't have Jesus or the Holy Spirit within. He was under the old covenant where God's presence would come and go. With Jesus and the Holy Spirit co-laboring with us, how much more can we do than what Nehemiah did? Can you imagine all the things that would be different in our world if families operated in this fashion? Or our church congregations, local governments, and national government? Our responsive obedience to what God asks us to do when we are in raw, authentic, intimate relationship with Him is what will open the door to us doing the greater things He desires for us.

Prayer: "Father, thank you for the testimony of Nehemiah and for the gift of Jesus and your Holy Spirit who empower me for the kingdom. I want to honor and serve you and only you, Father. Forgive me, I ask, in Jesus' name, for my sins, and I invite you, Holy Spirit, to help me change my habits so I can no longer go on sinning, but be transformed by the presence of Christ Jesus within me. Help me to see any place of rebellion or sin against you in my life so I can confess and be restored to you. Thank you, Jesus, for standing in the gap for me and making a way for me to be in relationship with the Father. Help me to honor what you did for me. Help me to remain in your peace despite my circumstances. Isaiah 26:3 says, 'You will keep in perfect peace those whose minds are steadfast, because they trust in you.' I trust you, Father. Amen."

Chapter 8

Understanding How Satan Works

If we are going to be successful in our journey with the Lord Jesus, we need to know who our adversary is. We need to understand how he thinks and what kind of authority he has and doesn't have. Conversations in the church about Satan tend to be very minimal and usually leave Christians feeling fearful of him. In Christ Jesus, we are not to fear Satan and his demons or the blows they may send.

Matthew 10:25–26 (NIV) says, "It is enough for students to be like their teachers, and servants like their masters. If the head of the house has been called Beelzebul, how much more the members of his household! So do not be afraid of them, for there is nothing concealed that will not be disclosed, or hidden that will not be made known." Jesus wants you to know that, in Him, you are armed with everything you need to stand against your adversary. You just need to learn how to effectively use what Jesus has given you.

Second Corinthians 2:11 (KJV) says, "Lest Satan should get an advantage of us: for we are not ignorant of his devices." Satan was created by God to be a heavenly angel. By his own free will, Satan chose to reject and lead a rebellion against God. Ezekiel 28:15 (NIV) tells us, "You were blameless in your ways from the day you were created till wickedness was found in you." God did not create Satan to be evil; Satan chose evil when he chose to rebel against God.

Demons are the fallen angels who followed Satan in his rebellion. Satan and his fallen angels were defeated and were cast out of heaven as punishment for their rebellion against God (Revelation 12:9, Luke 10:18) and he and those who followed him were hurled to the earth (Revelation 12:9) and ultimately are condemned to hell (Matthew 25:41). Hell was established to hold Satan and his demons. Today, those demons serve Satan and his plot for control on earth by luring man away from God. God desires that none perish, and He gave us a path to eternal life with Him through Jesus. However, the hard truth that is not culturally acceptable is that those who have not sought forgiveness in Christ will spend eternity with the one they serve, in hell, separated from God. Our eternal destination is not determined by good people or bad people. It is about forgiven people or unforgiven people.

The Bible describes demons as "impure spirits" (Mark 1:27, NIV), "deceiving spirits" (1 Kings 22:23, NIV), "the powers of this dark world," "the spiritual forces of evil" (Ephesians 6:12, NIV), and Satan's "angels" (Revelation 12:9). The Bible also tells us Satan and his demons can inflict harm on earth by possessing people to cause them both physical and spiritual harm (Matthew 12:22, Mark 5:1–20). Demons blind the minds of unbelievers so they cannot see the light of the gospel (2 Corinthians 4:4), deceive people by disguising themselves as "servants of righteousness" (2 Corinthians 11:14–15), promote false doctrine (1 Timothy 4:1), perform signs to deceive humans (Revelation 16:14), and torment believers (2 Corinthians 12:7).

Satan is not like God. Satan is not omnipotent, but rather, he has limited power. Satan is not omnipresent. He cannot be everywhere at once. Satan is not omniscient, as he does not know everything. Since he cannot do and know all things, Satan uses demons to accomplish his plans on earth. False gods identified in the Bible, like Baal, Moloch, Chemosh, and the Babylonian, Canaanite, and Egyptian gods, were demonic spirits that stood behind the shrines and idols and received the worship man offered. Satan loves to be worshiped and works hard to get people to displace their worship of the one true, holy God in exchange for worship of anything else. Matthew 4:9 (ESV) says, "And he said to Him, 'All these things I will give you, if you will fall down and worship me.'"

When the groups who openly worshiped those false gods died off, the spirits attached to them did not die. Our flesh will one day die, but our spirits will never die. Similarly, those demonic spirits also didn't die. Today, they are still active in the spirit realm and have persuaded many around the globe to continue worshiping them, directly or indirectly. Baal is one example of this (Jeremiah 7:9, 1 Kings 18:21). Additionally, there are humans in Scripture who, influenced by demonic spirits, rebelled against God. Their spirits went to serve the master they served while on earth, Satan, and they are now being used in his demonic armies. Jezebel is an example of this (see below).

Ephesians 6:12 (KJV) says, "For we wrestle not against flesh and blood, but against principalities, against powers, against the rulers of the darkness of this world, against spiritual wickedness in high places."

Principalities, according to the Hebrew definition, represent origin, the first in a series, principle rule, at head place, and angels and demons. If we believe a lie about ourselves and allow it to influence our thoughts and behaviors, we are putting the lie, and the principality that spoke it to us, first in our head. Doing this displaces God and His truth. Successfully resisting Satan and his principalities requires submission to God. We can try to resist him without submission to God, but we will find it doesn't work. That open door through our sin remains for Satan to walk through and establish strongholds as long as we have not submitted to God. Everything is relational in the kingdom, and Satan knows that. Without intimacy with God, things like hatred, bitterness, and selfishness will rule in our hearts, giving Satan an open door. And he will take it. He comes to steal, kill, and destroy—not just in the world, but also in your life. Relationship with Jesus is one-on-one, and He faithfully meets you in skinny jeans, right where you are. So why would we think that Satan isn't also operating in a one-on-one approach, setting out to destroy that togetherness and dealing blows with any opportunity we give him? John 10:10 (NIV) says, "The thief comes only to steal and kill and destroy; I have come that they may have life, and have it to the full."

Principalities serve Satan by being a spiritual inhibitor for believers and nonbelievers alike. A prominent example in Western culture today is the Jezebel spirit. Revelation 2 offers us insight about Jezebel the principality. In verse 20 (NIV), Jesus says, "Nevertheless, I have this against you: You tolerate that woman Jezebel, who calls herself a prophet. By her teaching she misleads my servants into sexual immorality and the eating of food sacrificed to idols." Jesus says to stop tolerating the Jezebel spirit. In diminishing the reality of its influence and ignoring it, we tolerate it and put ourselves in direct disobedience to what Jesus has asked the church to do. The influence of Jezebel in culture is like a contagion, and Jesus is calling us, the church, to stop tolerating it. Knowing more about Jezebel the person will help you understand more about what the Jezebel spirit's grip on society looks like.

Jezebel is commonly depicted in Hollywood as a power-hungry, fleshly, demonic woman who promotes sexual immorality and undermines ministry. Those things are true about Jezebel, but that is not all we need to know about the Jezebel spirit. This spirit is a high-ranking demonic spirit that has other spirits under it and uses men and women to lead others astray, to bring gossip, to lie, and to speak demonic prophecy into people and the world. Its goal is to harass the work of God, causing strife with its words and actions.

The Jezebel spirit draws attention to self, rather than to God. It moves by emotions and feelings, and establishes a perceived virtue and ethic attached to those selfishly rooted emotions. The Jezebel spirit creates division and drives wedges within the church and between leaders. Jezebel the human was the high priestess for Asherah worship among the Phoenicians. She hated God and had no respect for Him, or His prophets. She oppressed her people and abused her authority so she could get her own way. She attacked God's people, killed his leaders, and promoted agendas that were rebellious against God. Through those agendas, Jezebel established mandates against God and an idolatrous culture, and she stole from God's people. Jezebel tyrannized the people of Judah while she and her husband, Ahab, the king of Israel, funded false doctrine and engaged in worship of Asherah and Molec —the gods under Baal, who command child sacrifice.

Jezebel was rejected by her worldly father (Ithobaal I of Tyre), who gave her to Ahab in marriage to form an alliance. She did not want to marry Ahab. In response to the wounding from that rejection, she sought to avoid further rejection and began controlling everything and everyone around her. Today, many who are influenced by the Jezebel spirit have a story of rejection, often by their father in childhood. They also often have a dominant mother.

The goal of the Jezebel spirit is to get people with godly authority to disqualify themselves through defilement, inwardly or outwardly, so they cannot fully receive the ministry God wants for them. Since the entire church has godly authority in Christ Jesus, that means the entire church is a target.

In pure God style, He gives us the testimony of others to deepen our understanding of how the church can be influenced by Jezebel. Elijah, a prophet of the Lord who moved in intimacy with the Father, encountered Jezebel and was affected by her influence. We can learn from his experience in 1 Kings 19. I encourage you to also read chapter 18 for full context.

Elijah was a man of God and had just taken out hundreds of false prophets by the glory of God. Ahab witnessed the glory of God and told Jezebel about it. Jezebel responded by telling Elijah she was coming after him. Despite what God just did for and through Elijah, he experienced a profound emotion and reacted to Jezebel by running in fear. Keep in mind, the Jezebel spirit will try to diminish our godly authority, to make us fear, and to get us to run from what God asks us to do. She was successful in doing this to Elijah at this moment.

Verse 3 (NIV) tells us that "Elijah was afraid and ran for his life." Solitude is getting alone with God. Isolation is getting alone with yourself. Solitude is necessary—we need time alone with God. Jesus needed it too, as it's part of an intimate relationship with the Father. When the Jezebel spirit attacks, rather than running into solitude with the Lord, people tend to withdraw, get alone with themselves, and remain isolated. This is a dangerous place to be.

In verse 4 (NIV), Elijah became depressed and suicidal, and he prayed that he might die. "I have had enough, Lord," he said. "Take my life; I am no better than my ancestors." The Jezebel spirit will try anything to draw us out of God's plan, including depression and suicide. If it cannot take people out through isolation, depression, or fear, it will try to convince people to take a permanent step and kill themselves.

Then, Elijah slept. He slept enough to be restored. Out of a deep sleep, an angel awoke him to eat God's provision for him—bread and water. God first addressed Elijah's physical needs. He ate and then laid down and slept again, increasing his physical restoration. In verses 7–9 "The angel returned and touched him, saying, 'Get up and eat, for the journey is too much for you.' So he got up and ate and drank again. Strengthened by that food, he traveled forty days and forty nights until he reached Horeb, the mountain of God." God knew exactly what Elijah needed to come out of the spiritual influences of Jezebel.

Elijah loved the Lord and witnessed His glory, yet he was still affected by Jezebel the person. Similarly, the Jezebel spirit can affect even those who love the Lord today. We have an invitation in Christ Jesus to be part of honoring Jesus' prophecy in Revelation and stop the influence of the Jezebel spirit. When we choose this partnership with Jesus, we're choosing to stop tolerating the Jezebel spirit and the cultural acceptance around it, frustrate Satan's plans, and become part of ushering in the plans of the kingdom of God.

God loves us so much that He is going before us and warning us of Satan's schemes through Jezebel, other principalities, and the consequences associated with coming into agreement with them. This is, and will be, a common sin in the church, as well as in leaders who attach God's name to their platforms.

God cannot use us to the fullness He desires if we tolerate the demonic. He will remove from their assignments those who do. This sin may also result in a loss of anointing. God is reminding you that He loves to bless you in your obedience and that He has great purpose in the things He asks you to do and not do. He tells you, in Revelation 2:26–28 (NIV), that the person who abides and does stand up against the Jezebel spirit will receive the double anointing. "To the one who is victorious and does my will to the end, I will give authority over the nations—that one 'will rule them with an iron scepter and will dash them to pieces like pottery'—just as I have received authority from my Father. I will also give that one the morning star."

The only reason Satan and his demons have power is because the world tolerates it. When we stop tolerating it, Satan loses power. Don't miss that God uses the word "tolerate" on purpose. In culture, people use the words "tolerance," "embraced" or "accepted" as defining words for morality and ethics. Those worldly ethics look a lot like Satan: selfishness, control, division in the church, division among leadership, confused identity, child sacrifice (abortion), and sexual infidelity, to name a few.

In James 4:5 (NIV), James is talking to the Jewish Christians: "Or do you think Scripture says without reason that He jealously longs for the Spirit He has caused to dwell in us?" He is asking a rhetorical question to make a point. If we continue to live according to the world's wisdom, God takes that choice not to trust Him personally. He is jealous for the Spirit He has placed within us and won't easily allow us to live lives of self-service and self-reliance.

First Peter 2:9 (NIV) says, "But you are a chosen people, a royal priesthood, a holy nation, God's special possession, that you may declare the praises of him who called you out of darkness into his wonderful light." This is our identity in Christ Jesus. A royal priesthood, a holy nation, God's special possession. Our identity in Christ Jesus holds greater authority than anything of the demonic. Church, start believing and seeing yourself as God sees you and who He says you are.

Prayer: "Father, I confess that I have avoided learning about the spirit realm, that I have let it intimidate me into inaction. I ask you to forgive me for retreating from what you have provided for me. I ask you to help me change my habits, Holy Spirit, so I can be bold for the Lord and press into what is before me. Forgive me, Father, for tolerating the Jezebel spirit or any other principality or demonic force. Thank you for teaching me and for your grace as I learn. Help me to understand the ways I have tolerated Jezebel and to turn from them and toward you. Help me to represent your nature in the world and teach others what Jesus says about Jezebel. Help me to take up the command you have given. Thank you for your forgiveness; I receive it. Thank you for your delegated authority, Jesus. I want to know the fullness of what your blood has given me. Help me to learn. Amen."

CHAPTER 9

Conclusion

Ever since Satan realized that he did not actually win the battle by putting Jesus on the cross, he has been trying to convince the world that Jesus on the cross is insignificant. This lie is aimed at confusing the truth about Jesus so people don't receive it. Many died on Roman crosses. The ground was blood-soaked. Why was Jesus different? First Corinthians 15:3–4 (NIV) says, "For what I received I passed on to you as of first importance: that Christ died for our sins according to the Scriptures, that He was buried, that He was raised on the third day according to the Scriptures."

When Christ died for our sins, He destroyed the work of Satan. Jesus became the promised answer to the human condition. There is not a single emotion, circumstance, or experience we will have that He cannot understand. That was an intentional part of the salvation strategy of the Trinity. When the Father allowed Jesus to be put on the cross, He had this plan. He needed to understand the human condition so He could be the abundant solution for that human condition. We see this demonstrated all the way back in Genesis 3:15 (NIV): "And I will put enmity between you and the woman, and between your offspring and hers; he will crush your head, and you will strike his heel." Only Jesus could destroy the work of Satan. Only the Son of Man, the Son of God, could do what Jesus did on the cross. The perfect, sinless, spotless lamb, sacrificed for you and me.

Jesus is our representative before God Almighty. It was crucial for Jesus to be fully and perfectly man to be our representative before God. He perfectly followed all that was in God's will. Different from Adam, Jesus was tempted, yet never sinned. Romans 5:18–19 (NIV) says, "Consequently, just as one trespass resulted in condemnation for all people, so also one righteous act resulted in justification and life for all people. For just as through the disobedience of the one man [Adam] the many were made sinners, so also through the obedience of the one man [Jesus] the many will be made righteous."

As the perfect, sinless human, Jesus was the only substitute for us. He surrendered His kingly titles and authority to be that substitute for us. Our rebellious humanity deserves holy and infinite wrath. It's not about how big or little the sin is, it's about sinning against a holy and infinite God! We cannot pay for that, but Jesus has done it for us. Jesus, the God Man, was fully and infinitely divine so He could be our substitute.

Isaiah 53:5–6 (NIV) says, "But He was pierced for our transgressions, He was crushed for our iniquities; the punishment that brought us peace was on Him, and by His wounds we are healed. We all, like sheep, have gone astray, each of us has turned to our own way; and the Lord has laid on him the iniquity of us all." Five hundred years before Jesus, this prophecy was spoken. Only Jesus is fully human to represent us and fully divine to resolve our inequity. If He were just a good man, His death would mean nothing. It's because He's the God Man that makes the shedding of His blood mean something. This takes us back to the Old Testament with the question, "Why the blood?" What was the significance of bloodshed as a sacrifice?

Conclusion

Leviticus 17:11 (NIV) says, "For the life of a creature is in the blood, and I have given it to you to make atonement for yourselves on the altar; it is the blood that makes atonement for one's life." Old Testament atonement through animal blood sacrifice was not effective as a permanent solution to our inequity. It had to be repeated by the priests yearly. In God's intentionality and attention to details, the Old Testament act of atonement was looking forward to Jesus as our atoning sacrifice.

Hebrews 9:11–15 (NIV) says, "But when Christ came as high priest of the good things that are now already here, He went through the greater and more perfect tabernacle that is not made with human hands, that is to say, is not a part of this creation. He did not enter by means of the blood of goats and calves; but He entered the Most Holy Place once for all by his own blood, thus obtaining eternal redemption. The blood of goats and bulls and the ashes of a heifer sprinkled on those who are ceremonially unclean sanctify them so that they are outwardly clean. How much more, then, will the blood of Christ, who through the eternal Spirit offered himself unblemished to God, cleanse our consciences from acts that lead to death, so that we may serve the living God!" (See also Hebrews 9:22 and 9:24.) Blood matters. He comes not to offer Himself repeatedly, but one time for all time. His blood is all sufficient. His atoning death and victorious resurrection constitutes the only ground for salvation for all humans. Jesus' work on the cross is the fulfillment of the day of atonement from the Old Testament (Leviticus 16:15–16).

First John 2:2 (NIV) says, "He is the atoning sacrifice for our sins, and not only for ours but also for the sins of the whole world." Jesus' sacrifice was not just another death; it was the beginning of a victorious resurrection. It's because of His resurrection that we know He is the God Man, not just a good man (Romans 1:4). All our hope is on this. There is no other name that Salvation comes through.

Acts 4:12 (NIV) says, "Salvation is found in no one else, for there is no other name under heaven given to mankind by which we must be saved." The greatest problem facing us as humans isn't lying politicians, war, famine, or disease. The greatest problem facing humanity is sin in all its various forms. The news will tell you about all the bad things and bad people, ignoring the root problem of humanity: sin. Jesus is the solution. He alone is our atoning sacrifice.

Romans 3:21–28 (NIV) says, "But now apart from the law the righteousness of God has been made known, to which the Law and the Prophets testify. This righteousness is given through faith in Jesus Christ to all who believe. There is no difference between Jew and Gentile, for all have sinned and fall short of the glory of God, and all are justified freely by His grace through the redemption that came by Christ Jesus. God presented Christ as a sacrifice of atonement, through the shedding of His blood—to be received by faith. He did this to demonstrate His righteousness, because in His forbearance He had left the sins committed beforehand unpunished—He did it to demonstrate His righteousness at the present time, so as to be just and the One who justifies those who have faith in Jesus." Justification is the legal term for declaring righteous in a court of law. Jesus paid our debt and declares us righteous before God (Colossians 2:13–14). To redeem means to buy back. Jesus bought us out of slavery to sin and is our qualified representative to our Redeemer (Revelation 1:5). Jesus is in perfect relationship with the Father, and we get to take up His righteousness

Conclusion

and come into right relationship with God. There are no works we can do on our own, only through Jesus, by faith, trusting and receiving all Jesus did for us on the cross.

Jesus was beaten and brutally killed for our transgressions. When He hung on the cross, the weight of every sin of every person who would ever live was placed upon Him.

Do you respond to what He did for you like you respond when something bad happens in your family? If not, you must ask yourself a life-trajectory-changing question: What is the state of my relationship with Jesus? Does His importance to me align with what He did for me?

God's Word and the truth of what Jesus did for you is supposed to change the way you see yourself and others. It's supposed to change the way you think and perceive and live your life. That cannot happen until you change the way you think about the Father, the Son, and the Holy Spirit. Changing the way you think requires transformation of your heart by the Lord Jesus. Transformation of your heart requires a willingness toward Jesus. There was a time when I didn't know this. Now I do because Jesus showed up in skinny jeans and met right where I was. He longs to do the same for you. Will you invite Him?

Once I heard, received and applied what Jesus taught me, He began to position everything in my life into alignment with heaven. The more I came to know Him, the more I became astonished with who He is. The more I observed how the Holy Spirit was working alongside Jesus in my life, the more I realized that what I thought I wanted, I really didn't anymore, and what I previously had no idea I could desire, couldn't come fast enough. I began to see that through His word, Jesus and the Holy Spirit, God was revealing His kingdom purpose for me. He taught me that if I wanted to understand His purpose for me, I also needed to understand His heart for all His children. Specifically, I needed to perceive the contradiction between the heart of God and the brutality of how millions of His children are treated in both the manufacturing industry and the human trafficking industry. He revealed His heart break for His children who are in both natural and spiritual bondage. In coming into agreement with God's heart about these injustices, I also came into agreement that the ministry with a storefront He was inviting me into was for this purpose—to usher in freedom for those in bondage.

Everything He taught me was brought together and summed up in the heart of Jesus Christ and what He did to bring freedom for all of God's children. Now, His heart is represented through Adored Boutique. He took my yes and positioned me to receive all that the Father had designed for me—to live according to the will of God, founded on the word of God, dependent on the Spirit of God, for the glory of God.

Paraphrased from Ephesians 1:3–15 (MSG), God adopted us into His family through Jesus Christ. He invites us to enter into the celebration of His lavish gift-giving by the hand of His beloved Son, Jesus. Because Jesus died for us, we are free. Not just barely—by the skin of our teeth—free. We're abundantly free. God thought of everything we could need, and He took delight in making these plans for us. Everything is brought together and summed up in Christ Jesus. It's in Christ that you find out who you are and who you are living for. In Christ Jesus, you find yourself positioned to receive everything God has for you.

About the Author

Emily Smith grew up in Wheaton, Illinois. She regularly attended church, Sunday school, and youth group and had incredible leaders who loved Jesus in her life. Emily married Rolf in the late '90s and moved to Grand Rapids, Michigan. She still resides there.

In 2013, Emily surrendered to Jesus in a way she had never before, and everything changed for her. In 2016, she took a step of faith and left her 19-year career in nursing to open Adored Boutique, a ministry with a storefront in Grand Rapids. Adored Boutique has provided Emily access to support dignified wages for women in vulnerable circumstances and to speak into the hearts of women seeking more of Jesus.

In 2019 Jesus prompted Emily to establish Designed To Be Ministries, (DTB). DTB is a teaching ministry that has mentored hundreds of women into the freedom and authority that Jesus' victorious death and resurrection gives to all who believe. Through DTB, Emily also publicly speaks at women's events and records on YouTube. She also offers one-on-one prayer and executive coaching to help men, women, and Christian business owners grow in freedom, faith, alignment with God, and spiritual authority in Christ Jesus.

Emily loves to write and speak about the truths Jesus teaches her, the evidence of His transforming love in her life, and the power of an intimate relationship with Him. Emily is blessed to step into every assignment He brings.

www.designedtobe.org

www.ingramcontent.com/pod-product-compliance
Lightning Source LLC
LaVergne TN
LVHW041950070526
838199LV00051BA/2965